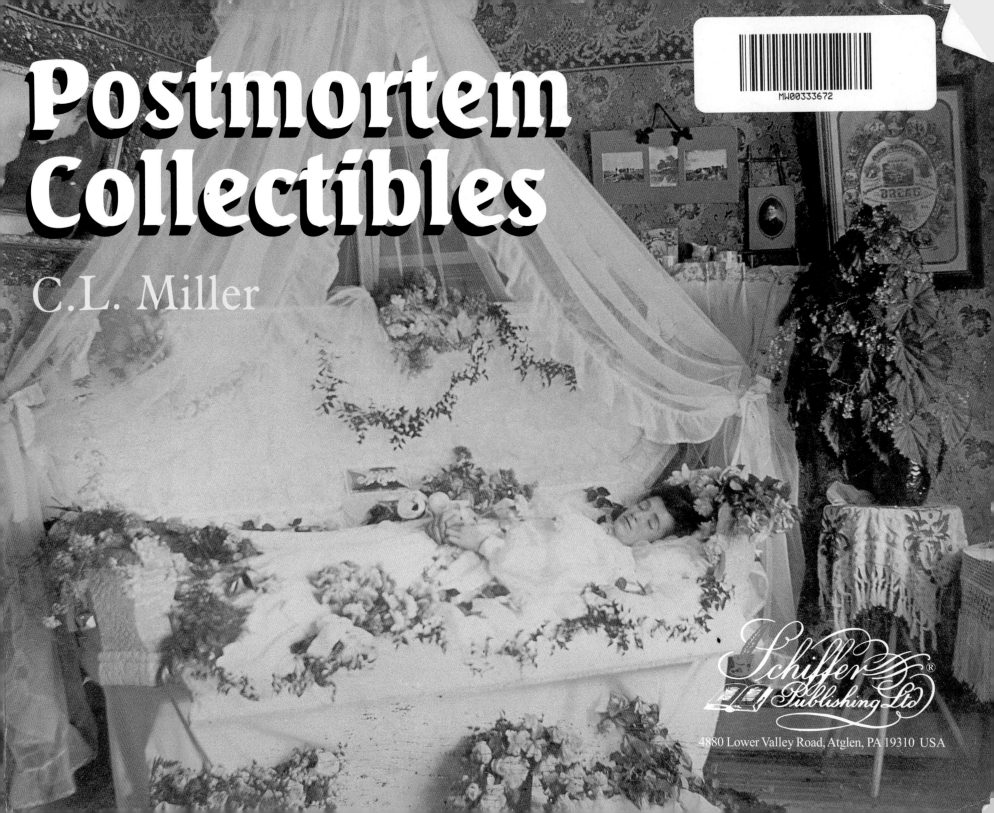

Postmortem Collectibles

C.L. Miller

Schiffer Publishing Ltd

4880 Lower Valley Road, Atglen, PA 19310 USA

Designed by "Sue"
Type set in Seagull Hv BT/Aldine 721 BT

ISBN: 0-7643-1330-4
Printed in China
1 2 3 4

Published by Schiffer Publishing Ltd.
4880 Lower Valley Road
Atglen, PA 19310
Phone: (610) 593-1777; Fax: (610) 593-2002
E-mail: Schifferbk@aol.com
Please visit our web site catalog at **www.schifferbooks.com**
We are always looking for people to write books on new and related subjects.
If you have an idea for a book, please contact us at the above address.

This book may be purchased from the publisher.
Include $3.95 for shipping.
Please try your bookstore first.
You may write for a free catalog.

In Europe, Schiffer books are distributed by
Bushwood Books
6 Marksbury Avenue
Kew Gardens
Surrey TW9 4JF England
Phone: 44 (0) 20 8392 8585
Fax: 44 (0) 20 8392 9876
E-mail: Bushwd@aol.com
Free postage in the UK. Europe: air mail at cost.

Dedication

"Until the day break and the shadows flee away"

To Robert James Stoyle (1952-1991) and to the memory of
those who in eternal sleep repose herein.

This paper "Funeral Cortege" sign was placed in the window
of a vehicle during a funeral procession during the 1950s. On
the back it indicates "You are No. 12 in Line and PLEASE
DRIVE WITH CARE." *Neill Collection*. $12-$15.

They identify you as part of the Funeral Procession. Use extreme caution while driving through any intersection.

This present day warning card hangs on the rear view mirror of a car, warning traffic of an approaching funeral procession. *Courtesy of Shirley-Kukich Funeral Home, Inc.* NFS (Not For Sale).

A funeral cortege in Salt Lake City. *Blackstone Collection.* $20-$25.

Acknowledgments

Without the contributions, encouragement, friendship and support of the individuals listed below, I could never have developed this project. I appreciate their assistance and confidence given during the development of this publication and if I have overlooked anyone, I apologize at this time.

Tony Alcosiba, Michael Alexander, Donna Baker, Editor, Schiffer Publishing Ltd.; Christy Bitler, Rod and Sally Blackstone, Bonaventure Cemetery, Savannah, Georgia; Joyce A. Bowen, Walter Daniel and Debbie Breeding, Evelyn L. Miller Cox, Colonial Park Cemetery, Savannah, Georgia; Paul David, Eliese Marcia Bodmer Chapman Davis, Susan L. Davis, Diane DiCenzo, Cynthia L. Donovan, Douglas B. Dupler, Dan Ewing, John and Dawn Fall, Floral Hill Cemetery, Hoopeston, Illinois; Dennis W. Frisby, John Gabel, Patricia A. Garrison, Green Lawn Abbey, Green Lawn Cemetery, Columbus, Ohio; Greenwood Cemetery Zanesville, Ohio; Susan Groves, Bill and Dee Hedges, Ronald A. and Beverly A. Koewler, Rose A. Kumfer, Lon and Lynda Lemons, Mike E. and Kim L. Lohrman, Donna M. Mahoney, Dr. Miles K. McElrath, Gerald and Kathy L. Messer, Mikelman Photographs, Michael A. and Carolyn R. McGuire, Mt. Calvary Cemetery, Columbus, Ohio; Cynthia Motzenbecker, Donna J. Myers, Old St. Louis Cemetery, New Orleans, Louisiana; Ken and Joan Neel, Linda Jean Neill, Antonette Raddatz, Mark and Debbie Raubenolt, James W. Shirley, Sr., Larry and Ruth A. Sigmund-Taza, and Jackie Weiner.

Special thanks to Pamela Rue Shirley-Kukich, Shirley-Kukich Funeral Home, North Huntingdon, Pennsylvania; Daniel W. Pallay, Director Cook & Son, Pallay Funeral Home and Crematory; George E. Chapman, retired Columbus and Central Ohio area funeral director and embalmer.

Foreword

This book has been written to emphasize the developing interest in collecting postmortem (after death or an examination of the vital organs made after death) photographs and merchandise related to the professional world of mortuary science.

Photographing the dead became popular during the early nineteenth century and continued into the late 1960s. Earlier tintypes, postcards, cabinet cards, daguerreotype, and Carta de Vistas (CVD) featuring the dead are also available to the collecting world.

Even today, with the availability of modern camera equipment and video technology, it is not uncommon for family members to photograph a deceased loved one in the privacy of a funeral home. This procedure is usually done after the majority of family and close friends have departed from the wake, funeral home, or place of viewing and is supervised by the funeral director or an assistant. While many family members are totally against this procedure even in today's society, it is often done to allow those family members who are unable to attend the funeral an opportunity to view the deceased and to allow a private moment of mourning and closure.

Postmortem photographs are the most popular type of collectible item related to mortuary science. Collectors search for these photographs in black and white, sepia tone, hand-colored, or painted, showing the deceased reposing in an elaborate casket and surrounded by elegant floral offerings. It is impossible to show or document every photograph or item related to this field of science, but readers will find a large number of representative examples depicted in this book.

A professional portrait is a photograph of the subject taken by a professional photographer (or artist) in which the subject has been posed and enhanced with special lighting. Amateur photographs are not as highly sought as those done by professional photographers. African-American postmortem is highly desired by collectors and has escalated considerably in price. Group photographs of family members surrounding the deceased casket or holding a deceased child are also very desirable. Children were often removed from their caskets and reposed against a bed-like seat, laid out on a couch, settee, or a divan. In many of these photographs, various objects, often a favorite item belonging to the child, can be seen in the hands of the deceased; these include dolls, teddy bears, fresh flowers, and even fresh fruit.

This publication is not intended to be shocking, gruesome, or offensive and is by no means a horror publication dealing with "the Grim Reaper." Death is a fact of life and faced daily by many. One should never view these photographs as morbid or revolting. We are all curious about death!

The original postmortem photographs shown in the pages to follow are not at all disrespectful. Many family members, indicated at the end of each caption, loaned their original photographs to be shown in this publication and wish to pay tribute to those who have since passed on and have not been forgotten. Many photographs were also purchased at local antique shows, shops, paper shows, malls, auctions, and household garage sales, as well as from private individuals and auction websites.

If you are seeking the morbid, the shocking, the gruesome or offensive, this publication is not for you, as it does not strive to offer that kind of subject matter. Readers should be forewarned, however, that some photographs are very explicit.

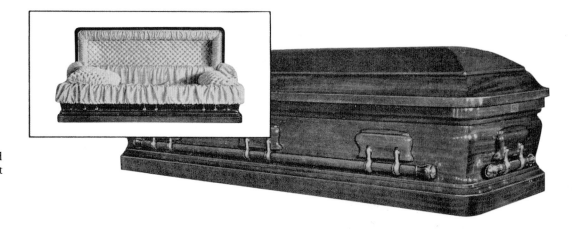

Original 1957 advertisements for a solid mahogany half-couch and hinged lid casket with velvet interior and mahogany polished finish hardware. Note that there is a difference between a casket and a coffin. A casket has four sides; a coffin, more popular in Europe, has six. Old casket and vault advertisements are available to collectors and reasonably priced. Advertisement $3-$6.

Contents

Introduction

Death is a subject upon which few individuals like to meditate but which all must one day experience. During times of bereavement we are faced with sudden and new responsibilities and with unfamiliar events to attend, and it is only natural not to want to think about anything pertaining to the passing of a loved one. Death is the eternal inevitability; the most real of all realities and the most difficult to face.

The suddenness of death, the sense of loss and grief, the bewilderment, and the strangeness resulting in loneliness, cannot be handled by many. They continue to grieve for the rest of their lives, feeling the almost constant heartache as a reminder. For many, the healing process allow them to become whole again over a short period of time; for others, no one can heal or cure the wounds of bereavement. Many seek assistance from support groups or bereavement counseling.

Many of us were raised alongside a strong matriarchal grandmother and/or parents who taught us "to never fear the dead . . . but the living." It was at their side that many of us placed our small hand on our first corpse, and later, with no apprehension, kissed the forehead of a departed family member.

Most of us have been present at numerous deathwatches (a vigil kept with the dead or dying), wakes (a watch held over the body of a dead person prior to burial), and funeral homes, or served as pallbearers for family, friends, and classmates. Young ladies may have served as flowergirls, whose function was to remove floral arrangements once the service had concluded and before the casket was carried to the funeral hearse (this procedure is no longer used in many funeral homes). Those selected were often family members or close friends of the deceased.

As we grew older we may have been asked to serve as honorary pallbearers, walking directly behind the casket of a friend while his or her grandchildren served as selected pallbearers. We may have stood at attention at the military grave sites of family members or viewed a deceased family member in the living room of their country farmhouse; this practice was once very popular. Many of us have witnessed the final hour when a loved one has been taken away. We try to prepare ourselves for that final departure, but often find that, no matter how strong we may think we are . . . we are never prepared for death.

For many it is a morbid, creepy, or gruesome subject and it is only natural that we, as humans, do not want to think about or discuss anything pertaining to the death of a loved one. Many others, however, have never been fearful or uncomfortable when discussing the subject of death or postmortem; we were taught to be respectful and reverent in the presence of the deceased. We were instructed never to walk across a grave or steal from the dead; we spoke in low tones when in the presence of the deceased or at a cemetery or grave site. It was unheard of and was not tolerated by the matriarch or our parents if we got out of line during a funeral, and this practice has been continued by many parents and elders. Death is as much a part of life as living and once death takes place, most religions teach us that this is the time you once again begin living.

Within the past few years, I have witnessed the collecting of mortuary science and postmortem related merchandise grow increasingly popular. The range of collectible merchandise related to this subject matter is constantly expanding and today we see a great demand among people of all ages—from the younger generations to those well into their golden years. It is often said "The older we get, the more emotional we become."

Postmortem photographs have become the number one rage among collectors of this subject. From the elaborate to the very simple, these photographs are highly sought and in demand, which has resulted in a broad price range due, in part, to specific geographical locations and subject matter variances. The cost of purchasing a postmortem photograph can range from $5.00 up to $1,200.00. This price range comprises a large classification of photographs; presently African-American postmortem has escalated in both price and demand.

Many collectors are only interested in photographs where the casket lid is open and/or removed to expose the body. There are two categories related to caskets: a half-couch refers to a lid open only half way and a whole-couch refers to a lid completely open to expose the full length of the body. Also popular are photographs of closed caskets where there is no exposure of the deceased. The more elaborate, unusual, and ornate the photograph, the greater the desire and price.

Photographs of young children and/or infants in elaborate layettes or burial gowns are increasing in value and demand. Many of these photographs are rejected by collectors because of the subject matter. The death of a child is a tragic event that often leaves the bereaved parents in an emotional shock. Women are often those who refuse to view postmortem photographs of children or infants.

Collectors frequently purchase photographs of funeral homes and places of worship. Interior views are much more preferred, however exterior views of edifices, suggestive of the time frame, location, style, denomination, and personage, may be desired.

Many collectors search for those photographs taken in a private residence, a procedure that was once very popular. Such photographs often provide a historical view of the architecture and furnishings of the period.

There is also a fascination with old photographs of funeral coaches, ambulances, limousines, hearses, and horse-drawn mourning coaches. The more elaborate and detailed the photograph, the higher the price. Photographs showing disposition of the body, walking corteges (which were generally confined to the poor), and committal services (committing to the ground) are all highly sought.

In collecting postmortem photographs very few can be found related to one deceased individual. If the services of a professional photographer were used, only a limited number of photographs would have been acquired by the bereaved family, thus reducing the number available to collectors of one subject matter.

Anyone visiting the eBay website, antique shows, flea markets, private shops, malls, tag sales, and even household garage sales, will have access to this merchandise—along with escalating prices. The demand has gotten so great that I recently witnessed a clash and overheard harsh words between two collectors. When the dealer refused to sell the item to either of them because of the conflict, they became verbally abusive to her and the photograph was removed from sale to the general public.

There are various organizations both in the United States and foreign countries associated with collectible mortuary science and related material, and various websites related to the subject have also been created.

This postcard shows the "Elmlawn" funeral car, built in 1895 for $5,798.00 by Brill. This funeral car burned during a fire at the Coldsprings car house in 1915. The card is © William Reed Gordon, Rochester, N.Y. $12-$15.

My private collection of postmortem photographs began with the family matriarch, my grandmother; three different views of her in her casket had been taken by a professional photographer. For years these photographs were kept out of sight and never discussed. After the death of my father in 1965, the three photographs were passed on to me. To date only nine of the original sixteen photographs can be accounted for. They are presently in the hands of family members or have been destroyed.

During my research for this publication I walked miles just to glean a bit of history about an isolated cemetery located off a backwoods road. I trudged through overgrown thickets in order to photograph a slab of granite or study a stone in some lone cemetery. I trespassed, scaling a farmer's pasture fence just to see what lay midway in his field, beyond the rusting iron fence that surrounded a solitary tree and a few noticeable monuments. There I found the final resting place of a family that had long been forgotten, except for the farmer and his "No Trespassing" sign.

In Savannah, Georgia, my favorite coastal city, I spent hours in scorching heat walking under moss-covered trees and among beautiful azaleas photographing elaborate monuments and statuary. I've watched nature at its peak as young foxes raised under illustrious mausoleums frolicked on green inclines and granite steps. At nearby stone-edged ponds and gushing fountains, wild birds, migrant geese, resident deer, and small animals drank and ate, having found an abundance of water, natural food, and safe refuge in peaceful surroundings,.

I've seen public and private family mausoleums that were in various stages of decay, sometimes to the point that vaults or caskets could be seen through crumbling and rotting walls. Behind massive locked and rusting iron doors and broken panels, I've viewed the deterioration of mausoleums' inner walls. Various public organizations are being formed for the preservation of many of these deteriorating mausoleums, as will be discussed later in this publication.

We have all seen monuments in such disrepair that the inscriptions on them could not be read. There are numerous types and variations of monuments chiseled with prestigious names. Classifications include "Children's," "Columnar Monument," "Cross and Cross Tablet," "Exedra," "Ledger," "Memorials of The Garden Type," "Obelisk," "Pedestal and Square," "Sarcophagus," "Screen," "Sculptured," and "Tablet." In a later chapter, many of these monuments of majestic height and breathtaking beauty are shown and discussed, along with various epitaphs. An epitaph is an inscription on or at a tomb or grave in memory of the one buried there; it can also be a statement commemorating or epitomizing a deceased person.

Some of the most sorrowful photographs I have taken are those of crumbling mausoleums, monuments, and weather-beaten stones that have been forgotten by families, or for which no living relative is available to provide continued care. Often it is discovered that an endowment was never established at the time of burial for perpetual care. (Perpetual care can be established by the family for continued upkeep and maintenance of a burial site.) Once the funds were depleted, many of these monuments and mausoleums began to decline.

We all have read of various forms of desecration to monuments, mausoleums, and cemeteries throughout the United States. This is one of the saddest and most disrespectful acts ever committed by an individual or group of human beings.

It is, of course, impossible to provide a listing or photograph of every cemetery and all the monuments that are located throughout the United States. I have provided those made possible through other collectors interested in this subject matter. Many photographs of monuments and funeral related businesses shown later in this publication were taken in Ohio and are representative of what would be found in other parts of the country (during the 1920s and 1930s, the midwest was considered prototypical of small town America). Postcards showing various entrances to cemeteries and/or views of cemetery monuments are readily available and presently inexpensive.

Cemeteries have become havens for both professional and amateur photographers, as well as those interested in genealogical research and gravestone rubbing. Many cemeteries offer self-guided walking tours and open invitations to the public to submit photographs of historic or scenic views to annual photo contests sponsored by local cemetery foundations.

Gravestone rubbing, which depicts the actual inscription on the head stone, is one of the most beautiful forms of gravestone artwork other than a photograph. This inexpensive avocation requires no special ability other than patience and good tools of the trade. There are various publications related to this subject, as well as informative websites. In addition, numerous genealogical societies offer classes in gravestone rubbing.

Most tools required for gravestone rubbing can be purchased at a local art supply, hardware, or crafts store. Required tools and materials include a soft brush that is not bulky in your hand (I have been told it is a wise to purchase three to four brushes to have available); a good grade of rice paper and/or tombstone rubbing paper; white, black, or gray chalk or rubbing wax; fixative spray; masking tape; scissors; soft absorbent rags; and small spray water bottle. There are firms that offer a complete gravestone rubbing kit containing all the essential tools.

It is wise to remember that gravestone rubbing is a way to record and preserve family history; once you have located the monument, approach it with all respect and honor. If the cemetery you are visiting is on private property or a municipal cemetery, it is always prudent to contact the property owner or the cemetery office (or seek out the sexton of the property, if such is available) and advise of your intention.

Often cemeteries will post warnings against "gravestone rubbing" and instruct individuals to take only photographs. If no notice is posted, it is still wise to seek permission.

Some time ago I observed a young gravestone rubber, seated on a small canvas camp stool at the base of a large granite monument. Her tools were carefully arranged in what I assumed to be a plastic tool box at her side. Using a selection of soft brushes, she began removing surface dirt and debris from the stone's surface. Once this was completed satisfactorily, the surface was sprayed with water and gently wiped with the rag. Leaving it to completely dry, she moved on to the next stone and repeated the process, then returned to the first stone. She secured rice paper in place, wrapping it tightly around the stone and affixing it with masking tape. Once the paper was properly in place, she began rubbing with a piece of chalk, starting on the outside edges and working to the center sections. As the detail of the stone began to form on the surface of the paper she applied a light coat of chalk spray. She repeated the procedure on the other stone that she had prepared, periodically checking to see if the first rubbing had dried. She then carefully removed both rubbings and trimmed each piece in the shape of the monument. There was no trace of her presence when she departed.

One of the most amazing experiences I've encountered occurred several years ago. I had the honor of attending the first public opening of the "Green Lawn Abbey," located approximately two and a half miles southwest of downtown Columbus, Ohio and a short drive from the entrance to Green Lawn Cemetery. This elegant, two-story structure, built in approximately 1927, has enshrined inside its massive marble walls, stained glass windows, and ornate iron work the famous magician, Howard Thurston, who died in 1936. Also located in the southwest section, in a separate anteroom, is the famous Sells circus family of Columbus. Other prominent Columbus residents are also buried here.

Shown later in this publication are photographs taken of this magnificent mausoleum. It is believed that the last interment was in 1999. Very little historical information can be found related to the construction of this structure. Only recently has an organization been formed to preserve and restore this beautiful mausoleum back to its previous grandeur.

Mourning Etiquette

It was common knowledge in the early 1900s that when an obituary appeared in a local newspaper, this was considered an invitation for relatives, friends, and acquaintances of the deceased to attend the funeral. In addition, handwritten and/or preprinted invitations were often sent through the mail (examples of these two forms of funeral invitations are shown later in this publication).

There were rules covering fine etiquette of mourning that were practiced during this era. Flowers were often sent on the morning of the funeral. Arriving at the house of the deceased early was unheard of—one would never go to the house of mourning until the hour indicated or published. A complete black wardrobe or a color as dark as possible would have been worn by the widow, parents, children, and close friends. A band of crepe worn about the arm was the mark of mourning for men. Women and widows often dressed in Melrose or Henrietta material trimmed with crepe. The skirt of one piece was plain, often had a slight train, and appeared to be entirely covered in crepe.

The widow's first mourning dress was worn for a year and a day and often she was required to have two different dresses. The second was a half-worn black dress entirely covered with rainproof material. The crepe on both selected dresses was usually revived because of daily wear.

Prior to the 1920s, there was an etiquette publication of "definite regulations concerning the period of widowhood" that provided the following: "For three weeks after a bereavement, women seclude themselves and receive no visitors except their most intimate friends. After this they are expected to be sufficiently resigned to receive the calls of condolence of their friends and acquaintances. They themselves make no visits until six months after the death."

"The length of the mourning period depends upon the tie which existed between the deceased and the bereaved. Except for an elderly woman whose husband has died and who never intends taking off black, the longest period is usually two years, the first in deep mourning, the next in 'second mourning' during which time gray, lavender, purple and white may be worn. This may be shortened to six months of deep mourning followed by six months of semi-mourning."

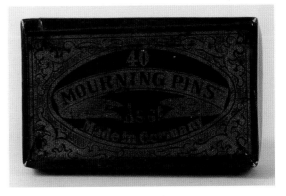

This carton contained forty black "Mourning Pins" made in Germany. These pins were used to secure black crepe material around the upper arm, indicating that a person was in mourning. *Neill Collection.* $40-$50.

In many of the older photographs shown later in this publication, various forms of mourning clothes can be seen, from those worn by the wealthy to those worn by the common worker. Society today does not set a dress code for a widow or widower, nor for those attending a funeral or viewing.

Today, unless a funeral is specified as private, everyone is welcome to attend. This is out of respect and for comfort and support of the family and friends. Condolence cards and letters, preferably handwritten, are sent to the family once others learn of the death. Families often request that instead of flowers, donations be made to a specific local charity or organization. The amount of the check is left to the individual sending it. The recipient organizations notify the family of the deceased and acknowledge receipt of funds. If flowers are sent, it is not unusual for the family to later acknowledge a floral arrangement by sending a personal thank-you note or issuing a public acknowledgment in a local newspaper. This practice is still being carried into the year 2000.

History of Embalming and Mortuary Science

Those interested in specifics of this procedure should speak directly with a professional or search for reference material related to the subject. Within this book, I will show various equipment, cosmetics, embalming fluid bottles, publications, instruments, and old photographs that have been made available to me. As noted above, please be forewarned that some photographs are very explicit.

Circle of Necessity

Once death occurs, a local funeral home is immediately notified. Those who have been entrusted with the care and preparation of the dead under enforced sanitary rules and regulations are often referred to as morticians or funeral directors. Their professional services commence when those of the physician end and continue until final disposition of the body.

Funeral home promotional memorabilia that was given away is available to collectors and presently moderately priced. Such items include yearly calendars, matchbooks, kitchen utensils, advertising brushes, thermometers, sewing kits, knives, ash trays and playing cards.

Final Disposition and Burial

Photographs of the final disposition and burial of the deceased are presently escalating in both demand and price. Usually taken at the grave site, such photographs are often difficult to find and not as available as casket views taken at a funeral home or residence.

Postmortem Photographs

Although specific photographs shown in this publication may no longer be available for purchase, this by no means indicates that postmortem collectibles are unavailable. In fact, there is still a large amount available for collectors. It is also recommended that readers refer to the Appendix ("Care of Collectible Documents") or seek professional assistance related to the care of collectible photographs and documents.

Services of a professional photographer were used to photograph the deceased shown above in a private residence. Some of the equipment can be seen in the photograph: to the right a special light has been put into place and the electrical cord is also visible. *Neill Collection.* $20-$30.

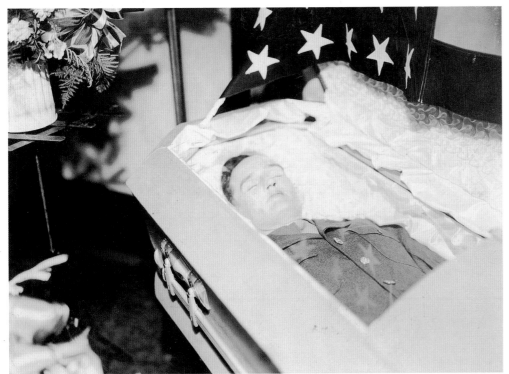

"Nobly he fell while fighting for liberty." A close-up of the corresponding individual shown above. *Neill Collection.* $35-$45.

15

Part 1

Embalming and Mortuary Science

This now private residence was at one time the "Dr. Buck - School of Embalming" located at 895 Dennsion Avenue, Columbus, Ohio. Historical information regarding the era of this "School of Embalming" is presently unknown. *Courtesy Bill and Dee Hedges*. Photograph NFS.

Author's Note: In keeping with the essence of postmortem collectibility, I will only touch on the actual procedures of embalming necessary to explain the various instruments, etc., that have become desirable in today's market. I do not claim to be an expert in this complex science. There are numerous publications and websites available for those who desire more explicit knowledge. Shown in this section are original instruments, fluid containers, assorted cosmetics, and other miscellaneous items that were made available to me for use in this publication. Because of the graphic details involved, some readers may want to slightly skip through this chapter.

The word embalm literally means to embalsam or to preserve a body by means of treatment with resins. The word embalm was derived from the Latin words, *in balsamum*. It was customary among ancient nations to preserve the bodies of their dead; much has been written about the mummies of Egypt and the sarcophagi of Etruria. Today bodies are preserved to allow a gradual drying of the organic substances, without the accessions of decay and putrefaction. Decomposition occurs by oxidation and dissolution, allowing the body to retain its lifelike form and color. The primary reason for embalming is for disinfection. In most locations, embalming is required by law only if there is to be public viewing.

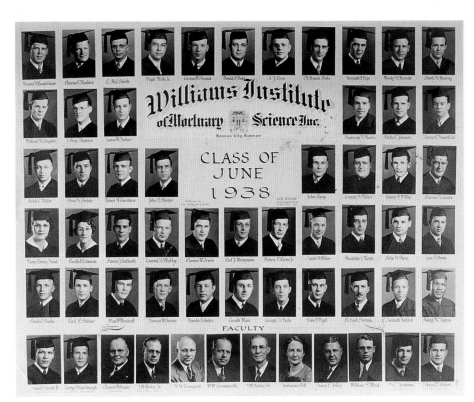

Students shown in this group photograph graduated from the Williams Institute of Mortuary Science Inc., Kansas City, Kansas in the class of June 1938. Institute President Clement Williams is shown third from the left in the bottom row, along with additional faculty members and the class President and Vice President. Photograph $10-$15.

Graduates of "The American Academy McAllister Institute of Funeral Service" class of September 1975. Photograph $10-$15.

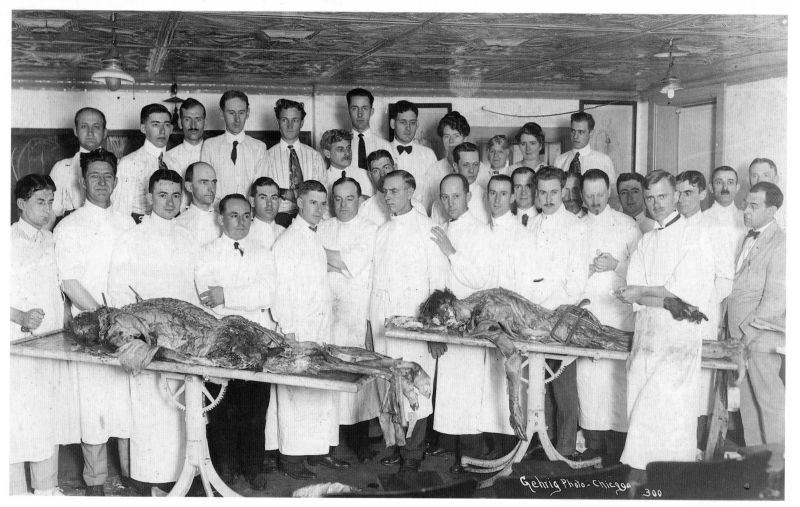

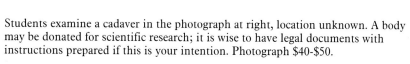

Students of mortuary science surround two cadavers on examination tables in this 1920s photograph, taken in Chicago, Illinois. Out of the thirty-five students and staff members shown in this historic 6-1/2" x 10-5/8" photograph, there are three women. Although the precise date that women entered the field of mortuary science is unknown, women have served in all positions related to this profession and continue to do so. Photograph $500-$800.

Students examine a cadaver in the photograph at right, location unknown. A body may be donated for scientific research; it is wise to have legal documents with instructions prepared if this is your intention. Photograph $40-$50.

Both embalmers and funeral directors require a license to practice their trade. States vary in their licensing laws and may require a license for each practice, as the function differs for each. In the state of Pennsylvania, for example, an individual who receives a license is both a funeral director and an embalmer, whereas the state of Ohio requires two separate licenses.

The funeral director sells his services—i.e., arranging and managing a funeral. He offers the customer a selection of caskets and vaults, and obtains burial permits and death certificates.

The responsibility of an embalmer is the care and preparation of the body along with all embalming procedures, including cleaning, dressing, grooming, and any restorative art that may be required to exposed areas of the body. When he or she has completed these tasks, the body is ready for viewing. "Trade embalmers" are also licensed but their main function is to travel from firm to firm where they perform only the embalming procedure. Shown later in this section is a traveling embalming bag with instruments that belonged to a "trade embalmer."

The Embalming Process

There are three reasons for embalming: disinfection (the primary purpose), preservation, and restoration to life-like appearance. Embalming permits the body to retain its lifelike form and color until interment and, depending on the success of the embalming, prevents decomposition in the short term and often indefinitely. Sentimentally minded individuals gain satisfaction from mental images retained after viewing the final remains of the deceased. This often provides consolation if suffering has been eradicated.

When a body is removed from a residence or public facility, it is placed on a gurney, covered with a sheet or put into a body bag, and taken to the funeral home. All bodies are treated with respect. If family members are present, they are often asked to leave the room or residence. Often this is left to the discretion of those present.

After being received at the established funeral home the embalming procedure normally begins immediately. Embalming is a most extraordinary procedure and can take approximately one to four hours of preparation depending upon the experience and skill of the embalmer, though this time frame may vary with different facilities. Proper embalming requires time and patience. Work that has been rushed may lead to facial swelling, which is impossible to correct. If this should occur, the deceased's family is the first to notice and often criticize.

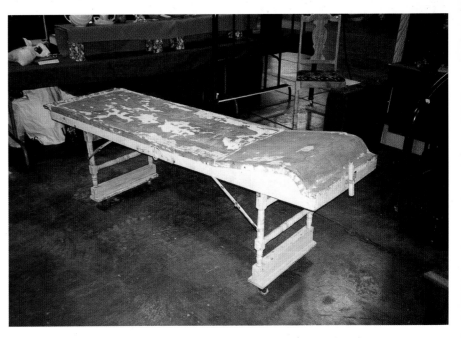

This embalming table was available at a local antique and flea market show some years ago. Discovered in a barn, this table could collapse for easy transfer to a facility or private residence. *Private Collection.* $200-$225.

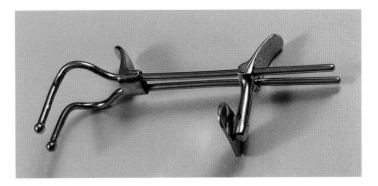

An early 1900s hand-held mouth clamp, used to close the mouth. *Private Collection - Photograph courtesy Mikelman.* $100-$125.

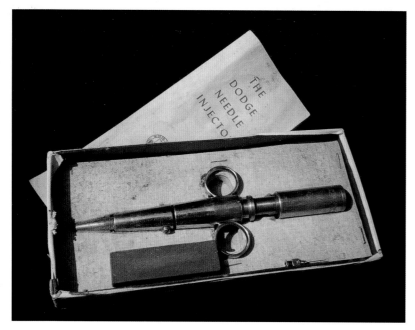

"The Dodge Needle Injector" used for closing the mouth. This 1950s set is complete and still in its original carton. *Courtesy George Chapman.* $150-$175.

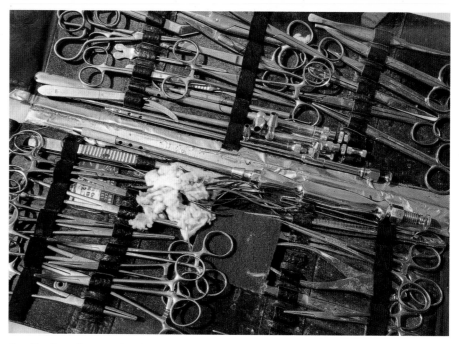

A collection of assorted embalming instruments, including scissors, needles, Trocars, and tweezers. These instruments were inside the embalmer's case shown below and date to the 1920s, 1930s, and 1950s. *Courtesy George Chapman.* Complete set $500-$800.

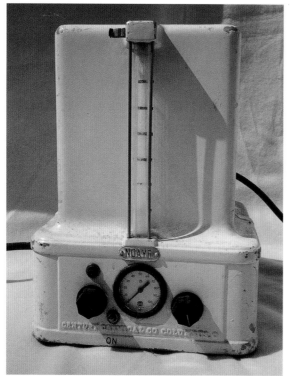

This leather trade embalmer's case dates to 1919-1920s and was used by a local Ohio embalmer. He would travel to local funeral homes, where he performed his embalming services. His business card noted that "Serving Funeral Directors" was his only business. Instruments shown in the corresponding photograph are still inside this case. *Courtesy George Chapman.* Case $100-$150.

Early 1940s "Pressure Injector" Champion Co., used to inject embalming fluid. *Courtesy George Chapman.* $150-$200.

The basic preparation of the body consists of a) placement in a proper position on the embalming table with arms at the side b) washing and disinfecting of the body c) removing, if necessary, any visible unsightly hair from the face, nose, and ears, including that of both women and children d) closing the eyes using small discs referred to as "eye caps" (shown later in this section), which are perforated and hold the eyelid in place e) closing the mouth via the placement of a "tack" in the upper/lower jaw (if dentures are worn, the denture is often fused unless the fit is imperfect and the look unnatural, in which case a plastic mouth-former is inserted instead) f) preparing the embalming solution and beginning the actual procedure.

An inventory of any jewelry or items that may arrive with the body is made, and those items are then turned over to the family. Glasses are removed before the process and replaced prior to public or private viewing.

Approximately three gallons of fluid and water will be injected into the body during the procedure, replacing the blood. Removing the blood is a necessary part of embalming, as doing so not only helps in the disinfecting, but removes the principal cause of disfigurement due to discoloration. A small incision is made where the largest circulatory vessels (carotid artery and jugular vein) may be accessed. After the process is completed, any tubes that have been inserted into the body are removed and the incision sutured.

The final step of the process is called "cavity embalming," in which an instrument referred to as a "trocar" is used to aspirate gases and liquid contents under suction and a preservative chemical is introduced. The incision is sealed with a "Trocar Button," shown later in this publication.

The body is again washed, cream is applied to the face and hands to prevent dehydration, the hair is shampooed, and the nails cleaned. The body is then covered with a sheet while waiting to be dressed and placed in the casket. Cosmetics are applied to replace the natural color removed by the embalming process. Cosmetics used by women are further applied to recreate the appearance the deceased had during her life; a woman's hair will also be combed and/or set. Adjustments are made to the clothing and hair as well as to the interior of the casket. The deceased's head and hands are placed in a lifelike position. The casket is moved to a viewing room or chapel for public or private viewing and any floral offerings are placed into position. After viewing the final remains of the deceased, individuals gain satisfaction and closure.

The body is sometimes reaspirated in case any circumstances are present that may cause a body to purge. Purging is especially bad if it occurs when a body is laid out for public viewing. The gases that have built up force body liquid out of the mouth and sometimes the nose. When this happens anyone present is asked to leave the room and the body is removed to the prep room, undressed, and reaspirated again. Purging is very rare, but it does happen.

It is not uncommon for people to donate their corneas upon death, and a process called "eye enucleation" then takes place. Some funeral directors take special training courses and are able to perform this service themselves: most funeral directors, however, allow the hospital team to take care of the procedure.

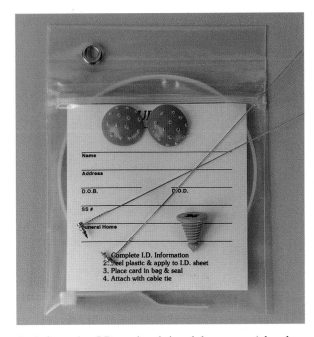

An information I.D. card and tie, adult eye caps (placed under the eye usually before the embalming process starts), cross slot head "Trocar Button," and mouth wires (which are injected into the upper gum and one into the lower gum, then the two wires are tightly twisted and the mouth is held shut). Items of this variety are often available on auction sites.

Embalming Equipment and Fluids

An older model embalming pump. One side allows air to flow in, the other is for suction. *Private Collection - Photograph courtesy Mikelman.* $150-$200.

Arterial embalming is a term that was adopted by the profession to differentiate between the methods of injecting fluid into the arterial system and draining blood from the veins. It is believed that the first to practice the system of arterial injection was Dr. Frederick Ruysche, between 1665 and 1717 in Amsterdam, Holland. Dr. Ruysche's work was so advanced that many of his colleagues were surprised to learn that the body was dead. After his death, Dr. Ruysche left no detailed records of his procedure nor of the materials he had used in achieving a natural color, pliable tissues, and flexible limbs of the deceased.

Between 1717 and 1783, a solution composed of turpentine and resinous oils was used by a Scottish physician, Dr. William Hunter.

Between 1728 and 1793, John Hunter preserved bodies by injecting camphorated spirits of wine into the arteries and veins of the deceased.

Another method, injecting a solution of arsenious acid with a small amount of cinnabar dissolved in wine through the common carotid artery, was practiced by M. Franchini's. Franchini's method kept the body odorless and in a natural color for sixty days.

A French chemist, Jean Nicholas Jannel (1791-1852), combined aluminum acetate and aluminum sulphate, which was injected into the carotid artery. Another Frenchman, M. Sucquet, used a solution of chloride of zinc arterially. M. Falcony would place the deceased body in a bed which he would cover with a combination of dry sawdust and salts of zinc (zinc sulphate); the body was then mummified.

Advanced arterial embalming was developed in America by Dr. Thomas Holmes, referred to as the "Father of Modern Embalming" in this country. During the Civil War (1861-1865), the United States government selected Dr. Holmes to oversee this procedure on the bodies of solders who had fallen in battle. This was for preservation only, as many of the soldiers needed to be returned to homes that were hundreds of miles away. The bodies were preserved but did not present a good appearance.

This procedure was not commonly accepted by the general public until the assassination of President Abraham Lincoln on April 14, 1865. Lincoln's body underwent this procedure and as word spread of the technique, it soon became fashionable.

The advanced technique of embalming by injecting chemicals directly into the circulatory system was first patented in 1856 by J. Anthony Gaussardia in Washington, D.C. Washington soon became the center of the embalming movement as competition and patents were issued for the development of embalming fluid.

Professor J.H. Clarke founded the Cincinnati School of Embalming in 1882, where instruction in anatomy and the art of injecting fluids by way of the arteries began. Soon other schools opened, by Professor Auguste Renouard of Denver, Colorado; Dr. Eliah Myers in Springfield, Ohio; and Dr. Carl L. Barnes, of Chicago, Illinois.

As the twentieth century approached, and as legislation had forbidden the use of metallic poisons in embalming, mortuary chemical companies began producing a formaldehyde fluid. Representatives from commercial manufacturers of this fluid were dispatched across the country to instruct undertakers in the use and procedure of this formaldehyde fluid.

By 1933, all licensed embalmers in the United States were practicing arterial injection.

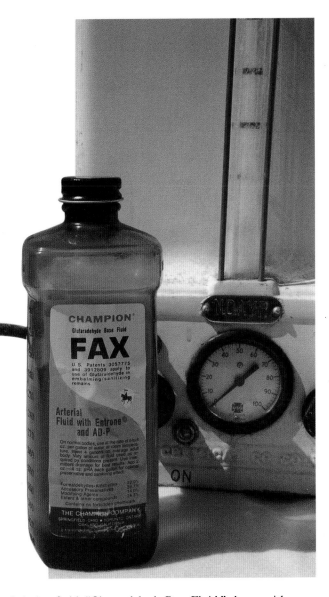

This postcard advertised "FIERO EMBALMING FLUID, Columbia Casket Co. New York N.Y." Date unknown. *Courtesy George Chapman.* $20-$25.

FAX embalming fluid, "Glutaradehyde Base Fluid," shown with embalming "Pressure Injector" machine. This is a plastic fluid bottle. *Courtesy George Chapman.* $10-$15.

Restorative "Rebuilds Tissue," Permatone "the Arterial Chemical," and Kosmol "the Pre-injection Chemical." From Laboratories of The Dodge Chemical Co., Boston, Massachusetts. *Garrison Collection.* $25-$30 each.

Vita Decker's Glow "Capillary and Tissue Lubricant." A Product of Decker Laboratories Inc., Colorado Springs, Colorado. *Garrison Collection.* $25-$30.

Champion® Cell Conditioner and Concentrated Non-Hardening Arterial Fluid Cosmetic Preservative. Made by the Champion® Company, Springfield, Ohio and Canada. *Garrison Collection.* $25-$30 each.

Frigid 5 Purpose Cavity Fluid and Eotex Arterial Fluid. "Compounded Only By Frigid Fluid Company, Chicago, Illinois." *Garrison Collection.* $25-$30 each.

Champion® Glo-Tone Arterial Fluid with Entrone® and AD-P. The Champion Company, Springfield, Ohio - Toronto, Ontario - Oakland, California. *Garrison Collection.* $25-$30.

Restorative Art

Restorative art is defined as "the care of the deceased to recreate natural form and color."

Egyptians extended their practices to the entire body remains and were the first people to practice any type of restorative art. They believed in reincarnation and prepared the body so that it would be in perfect condition for the next life.

In the United States and Canada, "Restorative Art" was developed at the end of the nineteenth century. Having no cosmetics, wigs, or instructions, the pioneers in restorative art first began using plastic surgery. After close observation they noticed that incision marks on the deceased could not be hidden and the practice was abandoned. Later, plaster of Paris was used for surface construction but also abandoned after embalmers discovered that it was difficult to mold and lost its proper color. Window putty and sculptor's clay were experimented with, as was cotton and collodion in surfacing; each resulted in the creation of additional problems.

Between 1914 and 1915, an embalmer experimented with yellow soap, which was melted and then applied for a surface construction—but a coloring problem developed. His next step was adding watercolors to white soap, which also proved unsuccessful.

Restorative waxes and cosmetics used on the deceased became available during the mid-1920s; as with the formaldehyde fluid, trained staff members representing manufacturers began offering demonstrations in the use of the products.

In 1955, a "Basic Course Content" in Restorative Art was arranged by the National Association of Colleges of Mortuary Science. Up till then, instructors had independently taught their courses through their own talents and persuasion.

Face Powder Brunette from Durfee, Grand Rapids, Michigan; and Velvago Pink and White Powder sold by Undertakers Supply Co., Chicago, Illinois. *Garrison Collection*. Face Powder $65-$75. Velvago $75-$100 each.

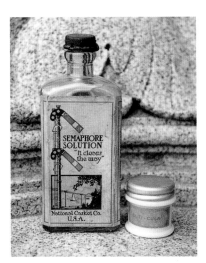

Semaphore Solution is "an aid to perfect circulation and better distribution of embalming fluid. Unexcelled for removing discolorations. Made of chemicals tested for strength and purity. No mineral poisons." Cold water was added to the contents of the 4-oz. bottle to make two quarts. The solution was mixed thoroughly and then injected through the artery, leaving the vein open for drainage, until both the arterial and venous systems were clear. This was followed by the injection of embalming fluid. National Casket Co. U.S.A. The bottle of Semaphore Solution is shown with a small jar of "Cuti-Cula," sold by Undertakers Supply Co., Chicago. *Garrison Collection*. Semaphore Solution $75-$100. Cuti-Cula $15-$20.

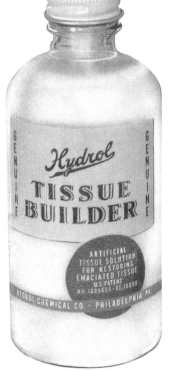

Hydrol Tissue Builder was used for completely restoring emaciated tissue. Circa 1950s. Hydrol Chemical Company Philadelphia, Pa. *Garrison Collection*. $20-$30.

Eye-Lip cement by Dominion. This early 1940s cosmetic was an invaluable preparation in sealing lips or eyelids and could be used to smooth surfaces in case of wounds or abrasions. It was available in either a small or large size tube, 6-tubes to a carton. Dominion Manufacturers Limited, Toronto, Canada. Original carton containing 6-tubes (either size) in pristine condition $100-$125.

Dominion Massage Cream closed the pores, left the skin toned up, and prevented chemical fluids from passing through the pores. This 1940s Massage Cream was available in either a 1 or 2 oz. jar and can be found in white or pink. Dominion Manufacturers Limited, Toronto, Canada. $40-$50 per jar.

This kit contained a hypodermic syringe and needle, three bottles of Dominion Renova, and one bottle of Cleaner. Dominion Renova restored the appearance of an emaciated body to the fullness of life, reducing the shock of death to family members and friends. It was available in 4-oz., pint, and quart sizes. Dominion Manufacturers Limited, Toronto, Canada. Complete kit in pristine condition $200-$225.

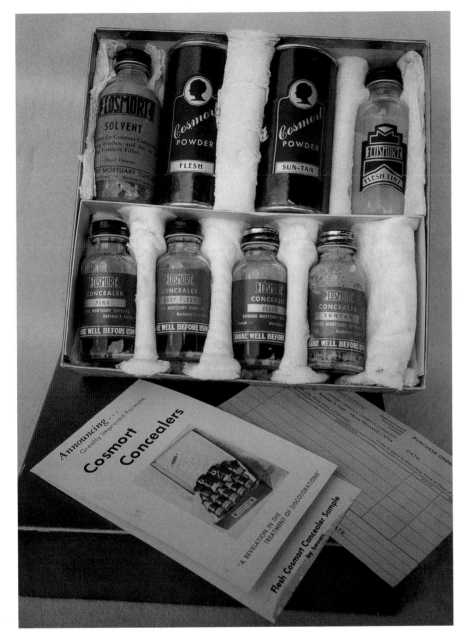

Left and above: This "Flesh Cosmort Concealer" sample kit was available during the early 1960s from Bowers Supplies, Inc. Berkeley, California. The kit includes Cosmort Solvent, Flesh Powder, Sun-Tan Powder, Flesh Tint, Pink Concealer, Baby Flesh Concealer, Flesh Concealer, and Suntan Concealer. Cosmort Concealers were a revelation in the treatment of discolorations. *Courtesy George Chapman.* $125-$150 complete.

If a body has been in an accident or has been discovered a few days after death occurred, facial reconstruction may become necessary. Wax is used for any place that needs to be filled in, built up, or smoothed over. Cosmetics are then applied over the wax to blend into the skin and hide the repair. Letheform Plastic Surgery Wax was available during the 1950s and was produced at the Century Chemical Co., in Columbus, Ohio. *Courtesy George Chapman.* $40-$50.

Part 2
Circle of Necessity

The Undertaker, Mortician, Funeral Director

The term "undertaker" was popular during the 1800s-1900s and literally meant anyone who, during that period, would "undertake" the management of details and who also provided funeral merchandise. The term "mortician" was popular during the 1900s-1950s. These terms are regarded as old, but many people still use them. Today, the politically correct term is "funeral director."

It is only human instinct to put unpleasant thoughts associated with death out of our mind. No one likes to discuss the inevitable end of life, but when it does occur, most of us are unprepared for such an emergency. When faced with this emergency, there are many decisions that must be made at once and most are made in an emotional state. By nature we are not calm nor are we thinking logically.

Immediately after death, a desired funeral director is notified. If death occurs at a public facility without a family member present, the family is notified of the death, at which time a funeral director is chosen. Many times instructions have already been provided to the facility in case of a sudden death. If death occurs at a private residence, the choice of a funeral director is still the decision of the immediate family. Regardless of the time, a funeral director is available at any hour of the day or night. Often family members will request the presence of their clergyman, priest, or a close friend as well. Once the desired funeral director has arrived, he or she will relieve the family and those present of the many details which arise—often those with which the family has a hard time coping. At this time, the body is enclosed in a flexible body carrier or completely covered with a sheet, placed on a stretcher, and removed from the place of death to the funeral home.

Under certain conditions the presence of a coroner is legally necessary. The funeral director who has been summoned will know whether or not the services of a coroner is needed and will make the necessary arrangements. Circumstances that require an inquest are usually cases of accidental death, death from mysterious causes, or the sudden death of a person recently under the care of a physician. If a coroner has been called, he or she may demand a postmortem examination and the family has no choice in the matter. A coroner does not have the right to suggest which funeral home should be called.

Once the funeral director has been notified and the body removed, details connected with the funeral director's services and legal matters are now in his hands until it is time for the selection of a casket, vault, location of interment (and/or cremation), type of service, and selection of burial garments. Surviving members or a member of the family must supply all necessary vital statistics to complete the death certificate, which is of considerable importance in settling death benefits under insurance policies. This information must be as accurate as possible and must include the full name of the deceased, birth place, birth date, occupation, place of residence, length of residence, name of husband and/or wife, name and birthplace of father, maiden name and birth place of mother, the date and place of interment. If an obituary is being placed in a newspaper, the funeral director will assist in the construction of this document for publication. Often family members of the deceased have compiled the eulogy.

Most families know or are referred to a local funeral director. In "small town America" usually one or two prominent funeral directors are known and/or available. Many are associated with family-operated funeral homes and have a long history of the business being passed from generation to generation. In major cities there are numerous funeral directors. Today, many of the smaller establishments are being purchased by corporate America.

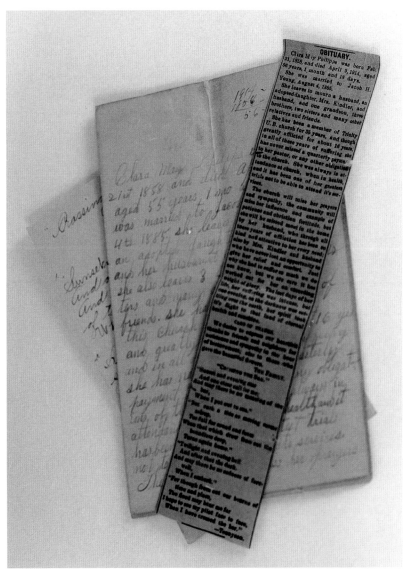

Original handwritten obituary and newspaper printed version for Clara M. Philipps, born February 21, 1858 and died April 9, 1914. Location unknown. *Photograph courtesy Mikelman.* $5-$8, both pieces.

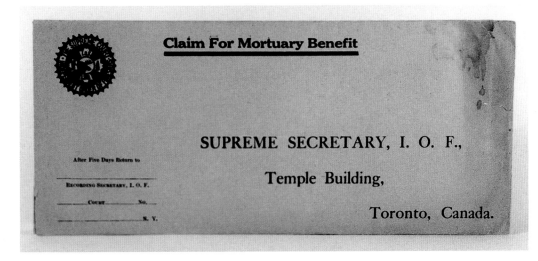

Claim For Mortuary Benefit

After Five Days Return to

RECORDING SECRETARY, I. O. F.

Court _____ No. _____

_____ S. Y.

SUPREME SECRETARY, I. O. F.,

Temple Building,

Toronto, Canada.

This envelope contains the "Claim for Mortuary Benefit" dated 1909. The enclosed Canadian documents have not been filled out and are for "Proof Of Death And Claim For Insurance Or Mortuary Benefit." The forms include a "Statement Of The Court," "Statement Of The Beneficiary Or Claimant," and "Statement Of The Attending Physician." *Photograph courtesy Mikelman.* $20-$25 complete.

This vintage silver gelatin photograph was taken in front of the "Zion Funeral Parlors, G. Wolpin, Undertaker." Location may be the Los Angeles, California area; the gentleman is not identified. Photograph $3-$5.

Large 16" x 12" photograph of the "Bevis Funeral Home," which may be located in the San Antonio, Texas area. *Blackstone Collection.* Photograph $20-25.

"T.A. Helms, Funeral Director and Embalmer," location unknown. *Courtesy Rod Blackstone.* Photograph $20-$25.

"Horrobin's Livery and Feed Stable, Undertaking," location unknown. *Courtesy Rod Blackstone.* Photograph $20-$25.

Postcard showing "Smith and Gaston—Alabama's Leading Colored Funeral Directors." Birmingham, Alabama. 1940s. *Courtesy Ann Davis.* $8-$10.

SMITH AND GASTON — ALABAMA'S LEADING COLORED FUNERAL DIRECTORS

Cor. 16th St. and 5th Avenue, North, in Down-town Birmingham, Alabama — Phone 4-3581

31

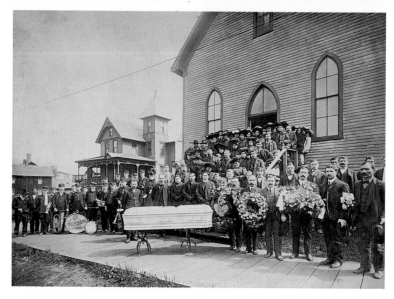

Exterior view of funeral with the closed casket in front of a church in Johnsonburg, Pennsylvania. Note the group of musicians on left hand side. *Courtesy Rod Blackstone*. Photograph $100-$150.

Exterior view of funeral home, location unknown, with pallbearers carrying casket to a hearse, surrounded by family, friends, and floral arrangements. A group of musicians play in the lower right corner. *Courtesy Rod Blackstone*. Photograph $75-$100.

Exterior view of funeral hearse and automobiles in front of the First Presbyterian Church in Boonville, Indiana. *Courtesy Rod Blackstone*. Photograph $175-$200.

Exterior view of a child's funeral, with open casket, in front of a church in East Toledo, Ohio. *Courtesy Rod Blackstone.* Photograph $100-$150.

Walking funeral procession in Canada. This may be the widow walking directly behind the funeral hearse. *Courtesy Rod Blackstone.* Photograph $35-$40.

Exterior view of circa 1920s Cook & Son, Pallay Funeral Home in Columbus, Ohio. *Courtesy Daniel W. Pallay, Director Cook & Son, Pallay Funeral Home and Crematory.* NFS

Exterior view of present day Cook & Son, Pallay Funeral Home, Columbus, Ohio. *Courtesy Daniel W. Pallay, Director Cook & Son, Pallay Funeral Home and Crematory.* NFS

Exterior view of Shirley-Kukich Funeral Home in North Huntingdon, Pennsylvania. *Courtesy Pamela Rue Shirley-Kukich, Director Shirley-Kukich Funeral Home.* NFS

Interior view of Shirley-Kukich Funeral Home, North Huntingdon, Pennsylvania. *Courtesy Pamela Rue Shirley-Kukich, Director Shirley-Kukich Funeral Home.* NFS

Grave site, location unknown, with hearse, driver, undertaker, floral arrangements, and two small boys. *Private Collection.* Photograph $75-$100.

A funeral hearse and lead car wait in front of a private residence for the conclusion of a service being held at the residence. Photograph $40-$50.

A closer view of the funeral hearse in front of the residence. Photograph $40-$50.

Funeral hearse, location unknown. Photograph $50-$60.

Spanish soldiers present arms as hearses containing the bodies of three journalists are taken across the Franco-Spanish frontier at Irun on their way to Paris, January 5th, 1938. *Acme Newspictures, Inc.* Photograph $12-$15.

World War I mounted soldiers present arms as pallbearers place a fallen soldier's flag draped casket into a hearse. *Neill Collection*. Photograph $40-$50.

Arms are presented as pallbearers place a flag draped casket into a hearse. *Neill Collection*. Photograph $25-$35.

The flag draped casket of Mary Baker is taken from the hearse. Miss Baker was an employee with the Navy Department, Washington, D.C. She was murdered in 1930 and her body was found in a culvert near Arlington National Cemetery. *Acme Newspictures, Inc.* Photograph $75-$100.

The back of this 1920s postcard reads "Uncle Earl's Funeral." Location unknown. *Blackstone Collection.* $12-$15.

Below and below left: A Canadian funeral cortege winds its way along a dirt road to the cemetery in these two photographs. The horse drawn hearse can be seen in the center of the funeral cortege in the second photograph. *Blackstone Collection.* Photographs $25-$30 each.

A flag draped casket surrounded by floral arrangements sits inside a Utah church. The back of this photograph is marked "Wages Funeral." *Private Collection.* Photograph $15-$20.

Uniformed pallbearers carrying the "Wages Funeral" casket from the Utah church. *Private Collection.* Photograph $15-$20.

Stratford Engine 2 Fire Department truck carries a casket past the fire station en route to the cemetery. *Private Collection.* Photograph $25-$30.

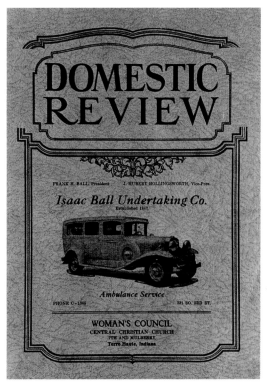

This photograph of a funeral hearse from the Isaac Ball Undertaking Co., established 1847, appeared on the cover of *Domestic Review*, a buyer's guide published for Terre Haute, Indiana residents. *Chapman Collection.* $12-$15.

Promotional Memorabilia

"Everyone in town knows me!"

Advertising is a way to reach the people. Written words and pictures draw attention to a business and once people notice, they remember. A funeral director advertises for the same reason any other individual or organization offering a service for sale advertises—because the public in general has to be informed if the business is to prosper. A funeral director or funeral home has to sell the public on what they have and what they can do. Everyone knows a funeral director or can name a least one funeral home within their community. Many of us pass such an establishment every day.

A funeral director who advertises shows the public that he has made the profession whole, he has advanced with the times and kept up with progress. The first such advertisements often appeared in large print on the funeral director's front window or across the front of his establishment, as shown in the photographs within this book. Newspaper ads also provided a consistent source of publicity. In many larger cities, posters, leaflets, handbills, and direct mailings were often used.

One of the most popular forms of advertising was the use of novelties. Often available to the collector and moderately priced today, these include thermometers, paperweights, letter openers, calendars, kitchen gadgets, ashtrays, china, matchbooks, cooking utensils, and fans. Calendars, for example, have been given out by funeral homes for years; they often displayed a religious scene along with their firm's name in bold print. Many funeral homes had difficulty keeping a supply available. For some funeral homes, however, novelty advertising did not pay. Many people found that receiving a novelty item from a funeral director was depressing and tended to bring up unpleasant thoughts.

Shown here are advertising items provided from my own private collection as well as from other sources.

Ashtrays, Mugs, and Glassware

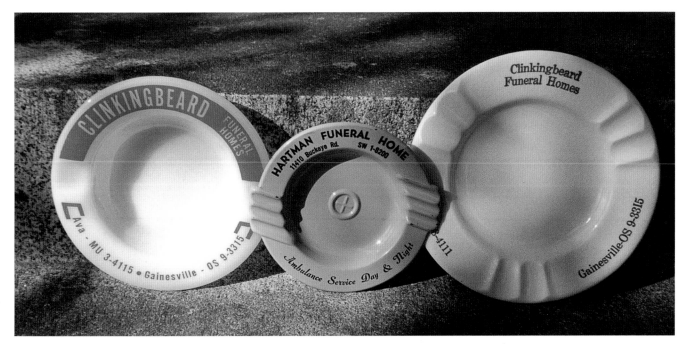

At present, ashtrays are plentiful and moderately priced. Shown here are three examples of collectible funeral home advertising ashtrays. Made of green enamel, china, and white milk glass, each receptacle is printed with the establishment's name, location, and telephone number. These ashtrays appeal to those interested in mortuary science as well as to ashtray collectors. *Courtesy George E. Chapman.* Enamel $10-$15, China/Milk Glass $5-$8 each.

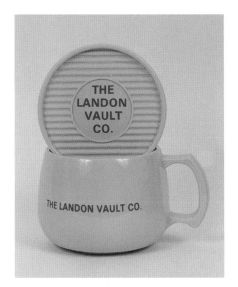

"The Landon Vault Co." plastic mug and coaster. *Photograph courtesy Mikelman.* $10-$12.

"Cocktails for Two! You - Me" was a promotional set offered by the "Baumann Brothers, Inc. Funeral Home" in Overland, Missouri. *Courtesy Rod Blackstone.* Complete set $15-$20.

A novelty "Pallbearer" mug. *Photograph courtesy Mikelman.* $5-$8.

Complete 1940 calendar "Presented by Reeves Funeral Home," Tabor, Iowa. *Courtesy George E. Chapman.* $10-$15.

Calendars

Calendars were issued annually from various funeral homes and burial vault companies. These documents that mark the passing of time are plentiful and moderately priced. Those that are older will demand higher prices and must be complete and in excellent condition.

This daily inspiration, "What the Bible Says," 1950s calendar was "Presented by Thompson Funeral Home," Mt. Orab, Ohio. This calendar is in mint condition. *Courtesy George E. Chapman.* $10-$15.

Pictorial Fans

Some of the most common promotional pieces were cardboard three-fold and single fans. Pictorial fans were available with various spiritual verses, religious pictures, or views of the funeral home. These pictorial funeral home fans are presently available and moderately priced. *Davis Collection.* $5-$15 each.

Kitchen Gadgets

This selection of kitchen gadgets includes a pencil, file, kitchen tongs, magnet, bottle opener and cap, tape measure, measuring spoon with bottle opener end, plastic kitchen draining utensil, and advertising matches. *Blackstone Collection.* Pencil $1-$3, File $5-$8, Tongs $10-$12, Opener/Cap $3-$5, Tape Measure $15-$20, Measuring Spoon/Opener $5-$8, Magnet $3-$5, Draining Utensil $4-$6, Matches $5-$10.

Memorial folders and "Memory Registers" or "Guest Registers" are popular among certain collectors. The modest register shown here was issued in New Berlin, New York in 1962. Written inside is information related to the deceased and a register of those friends attending the viewing or funeral. The "Memorial" folder was usually given out at the home (during home viewing) or available near the guest register at the funeral home. The "Memorial" folders shown here are for "Susan Gannon Died, Good Friday, April 21, 1916" and "Mrs. Mary Hale Haugh Died July 3, 1934 in Turtle Creek, Penna." Mrs. Haugh's card "A Memorial Record For Friends and Relatives" is ©1930. "Remembered in Love" is a large Memorial folder and is dated 1999. Prices of these Memorial folders, Memorial cards, Memory books, and Prayer Cards will vary because of significant geographical differences and preferences. *Photograph courtesy Mikelman.*

Publications, Periodicals, and Brochures

Collectors interested in the further study of mortuary science may check with their local library, bookstore, antique shows, flea markets, book fairs, eBay website, or one of the local book websites for reference material—there are numerous publications available for the scholar. It is impossible to show every publication related to funeral home history, cemetery history, and mortuary science. Paper documents are moderately priced at present and most are readily available, though not all of the documents will be available because of significant geographical differences. When a firm's name appears in print on any form of advertising, the item often becomes collectible—from a single page cardboard advertisement to a forty page brochure. The rarer the document, the more premium the price.

"To the honored memory of the beloved departed,
To the peace and consolation of the bereaved,
To the increase of faith and the strengthening of hope,
In God and life everlasting,
This token is dedicated with deepest compassion."

©Wendell & Co. Memorial Flyer, 1900

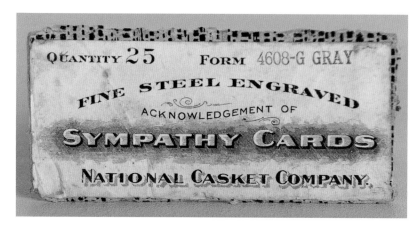

National Casket Company "Sympathy Cards." This carton held twenty-five sympathy cards. *Blackstone Collection.* $25-$30 complete.

"We regret to inform you of the death . . ." These announcements of a death were mailed to close friends during the late 1920s and early 1930s. *Neill Collection.* $8-$10 each.

H.F. Wendell & Co.

At the turn of the nineteenth century, memorial houses began springing up. These companies produced a variety of funeral memorial cards, testimonials, memento keepsakes, and related remembrances to ease the pain of losing a loved one. H. F. Wendell began his memorial business in 1888 and within three years his business was the largest of its kind in America. Wendell was the general manager of the business and for six years was the editor and publisher of the *Leipsic Tribune*. He twice refused the nomination for State Senator, but held the following offices: Vice President and Director, the First National Bank; Vice President, Townsend Oil Products Co.; President, Wendell Vacuum Washington Machine Co.; Secretary and Director, Dollar Oil Co.; Secretary of the Board of Trade; and President of the Law and Order League organized to promote the moral welfare of the city.

H.F. Wendell, General Manager of H.F. Wendell & Co.

Home offices of "The Largest Memorial House on Earth. H.F. Wendell & Co., Leipsic, Ohio."

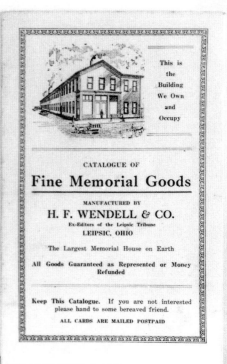

Two variations of "Fine Memorial Goods" catalogues that were available from the Wendell Co. These catalogues offered a large selection of sturdy cabinet memorial cards. Customers could select from various inscriptions and illustrations, shown inside each catalogue. Additional catalogues, flyers, pamphlets, and assorted brochures have surfaced related to the Wendell Co., since beginning this publication. *Blackstone Collection*. $35-$40 each.

"In Loving Remembrance." Framed 7-1/4" x 13" memorial was in remembrance of "Our Dear One Mrs. Laura C. Coldren Born Oct. 5, 1892, Died June 3, 1920. Age 27 yrs, 7 mos. 28 days." Her photograph is inserted in this remembrance picture. *Neill Collection.* $75-$100.

"Gone But Not Forgotten" for "Our Dear Father & Mother, John M. Rine, Died 1894 - Mary, Died 1890." This remembrance photograph by the Wendell Co. is 21-1/4" x 23-1/4". Customers could have their loved ones photograph printed on selected cabinet memorial cards and/or in larger framed portraits. *Blackstone Collection.* $100-$125.

"The Angel of Peace In Loving Remembrance Of Nora Solars Died January 15, 1908 - Age 9 years." Nora was my grandmother's sister; her last name was misspelled. It should have been "Sollars." NFS.

A child's photograph is inserted among an arrangement of roses and assorted flowers in this remembrance photograph. The back of the photograph is marked "The Wendell Co." *Blackstone Collection.* $50-$75.

48

Part 3
Final Dispositions

Caskets

Postcard, c. 1928-1932, showing the entrance to the Drake Casket Co., location unknown. *Blackstone Collection.* $45-$50.

This casket key in original carton was "Engineered For Maximum Protection." The key design is the same and works in all units, no matter which major company a casket is purchased from. The key has two functions: it lowers and raises the bed for proper positioning of the remains and is later inserted into the side or front of the casket to hermetically seal the unit. This makes the casket air and water tight. *Chapman Collection.* $15-$20.

Belmont Casket Co., in Columbus, Ohio. In 1956 the Belmont Casket Co. celebrated its 50th year as a manufacturer of caskets. One of the country's leading manufacturers of caskets, Belmont was founded in 1906 in Bellaire, Ohio with a two-man sales force. The contained growth of the company under the leadership of president C.W. Troll soon required the construction of a larger facility and distribution center, and in 1915 a new plant and center in Columbus was opened. During the 1950s, the factories in Bellaire and Columbus totaled over 245,000 square feet of space with an additional 30,000 feet of space added in 1955 to the Columbus facility to meet the demand for lead-coated steel caskets. Belmont pioneered and developed a new lead-coated steel casket. These metal caskets consisted of a one piece seamless top and were fully guaranteed to protect the remains from any outside infiltration. Over 40 percent of Belmont's employees in the 1950s had been with the company for twenty years or more. The facility in Columbus employed a staff of 250 and operated branch offices in Boston, New York City, and Mineral Wells, Texas, with 25 representatives covering the entire United States and sections of Canada. The Belmont Casket Company was located at 330 West Spring Street in Columbus, Ohio and ceased operations in the late 1950s.

One of the most important decisions facing a family is the selection of a casket. This is usually done after the funeral director has received the body.

Until recently, caskets and urns were only available through the funeral home. In 1994 the Federal Trade Commission (FTC) gave the right to individuals to use a third party casket or urn. This ruling also denied funeral homes the right to charge a "handling fee" or to increase prices of other services in order to make up for the high profit they were making on caskets.

At one time the most expensive metallic caskets were cast bronze and solid copper sarcophagi. These were often selected for burial of the prominent and wealthy. Not all metallic caskets were in the high price range, however; funeral directors often displayed those in the moderate price range. Hardwood caskets in natural finish or cloth-covered caskets were often selected by middle class families. Selection of the proper casket was often determined by the amount the family desired to spend combined with personal taste.

The embossed cloth covered material caskets are referred to as moleskin." Cloth was often seen spelled as "kloth." The surrounding material and lining inside the casket is for decorative purposes and provides a softer look than that of just a metal or wooden box. Some lining is padded and can be used for positioning of the body; this material is often crepe or velvet and can include sovereign velvet, twill crepe, and numerous others.

H.A. Neff, President of Belmont Casket Co., began in 1906 as an engineer and plant superintendent, having been with the company during its entire fifty years of existence. The exact date on which H.A. Neff became President is unknown. I have been unable to locate documents that would provide historical information as to when or if he succeeded C.W. Troll. The name "Belmont meant . . . Dignity."

NO. 7891

Original black and white advertisement photograph of the elaborate "Whole Couch" metal casket No. 7891, manufactured by the Illinois Casket Company, Chicago, Illinois. Photograph $10-$15.

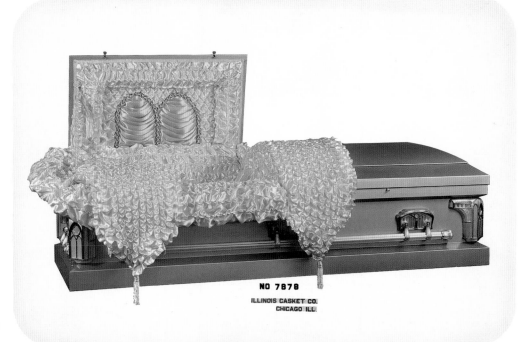

NO 7878

ILLINOIS CASKET CO.
CHICAGO ILL.

Original black and white advertisement photograph of elaborate "Half Couch" metal casket No. 7878, manufactured by the Illinois Casket Company, Chicago, Illinois Photograph $10-$15.

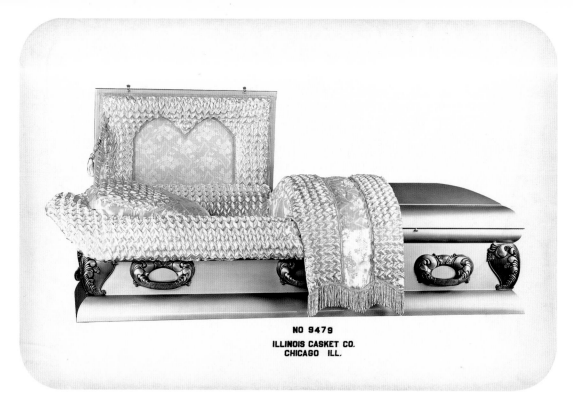

NO 9479
ILLINOIS CASKET CO.
CHICAGO ILL.

Original black and white advertisement photograph of another "Half Couch" metal casket with elaborate interior, No. 9479, manufactured by the Illinois Casket Company, Chicago, Illinois. The wholesale price for this casket as indicated on the back ranged from $83.50-$91.00 depending on the selection of the interior material and finish. Photograph $10-$15.

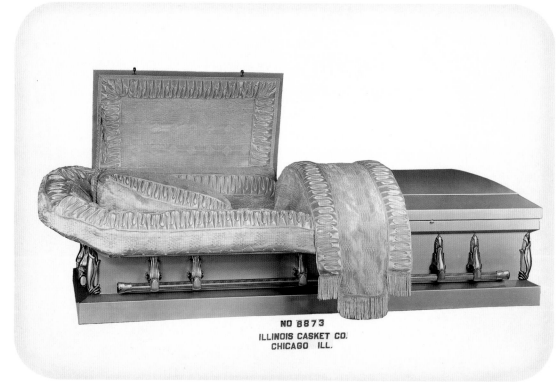

NO 8873
ILLINOIS CASKET CO.
CHICAGO ILL.

This "Full Couch" casket No. 8873 sold for $98.00 and was tailored in Frizze and Venus material only. Manufactured by the Illinois Casket Company, Chicago, Illinois. Photograph $10-$15.

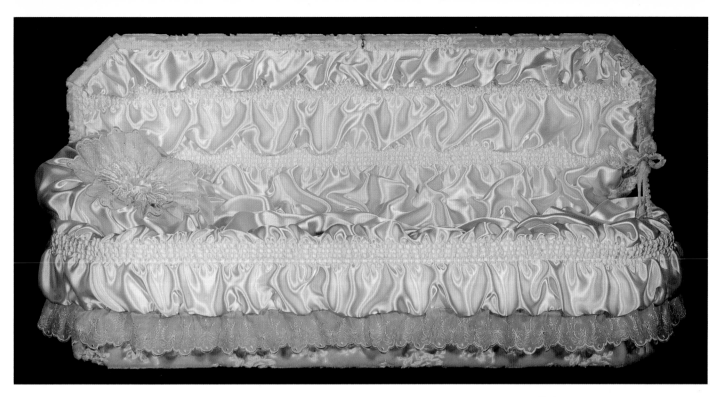

Left: Elaborate "Full Couch" child's casket, manufactured by a Sacramento, California firm. Photograph $50-$75.

Below: The original advertisement for this "Half Couch" casket listed it as No. 127 with "Picture Frame Colonial Crepe Ivory and Orchid Velvet Trim." Spokane location. *Chapman Collection.* Photograph $8-$10.

The original advertisement for this "Half Couch" casket listed it as No. 2720 with "Board Braid Colonial Crepe and Ivory over Peach." Spokane location. *Chapman Collection.* Photograph $8-$10.

53

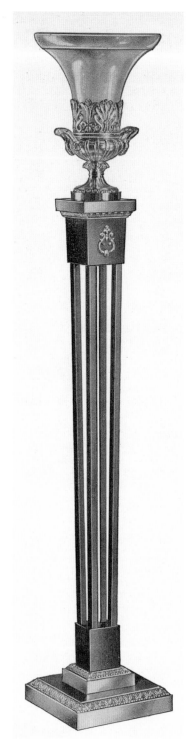

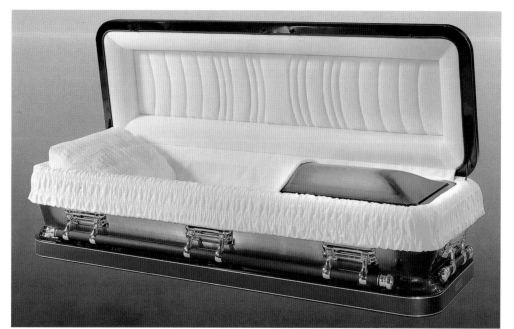

This elaborate "Full Couch" casket with a "Bronze Inner Panel" was resistant to rust and corrosion. It has a rounded corner urn design, 24-karat gold plated hardware, brushed finish, adjustable bed and mattress. ©1990 Batesville Casket Co., Inc. The Batesville Casket Co. is one of the leading casket manufacturing firms with headquarters in Batesville, Indiana. The company began in 1906 under the leadership of John A. Hillenbrand. More history on this company can be found at their website, www.batesville.com. Photograph $8-$10.

Left: They were advertised as the ultimate in quality, new in conception, flawless in execution and precision workmanship. Often referred to as a "Torchiere," these floor lamps were placed at the head and foot of the casket casting light upward so as to give indirect illumination. Highly collectible, these lamps have become very expensive in the secondary market. Price may vary depending on geographical location. $500-$1000 per pair.

Right: This large 13-1/4" x 9-3/4" photograph shows a closed casket surrounded by floral arrangements in various wicker containers and was taken at a private residence in Mitchell, South Dakota. It is marked "Aunt Claras Flowers" at the bottom and is an exceptional example of home decorating for that period. Note the piano, wall covering, pictures, carpet, and lighting. Photograph $45-$50.

Original 8" x 10" black and white photograph of a closed casket. The floral arrangement on top of the casket indicates "Beloved Husband." Photograph $20-$25.

Original 8" x 10" black and white photograph of an open casket with elaborate floral arrangements, taken in a private residence. Photograph $20-$25.

Original 4-3/4" x 6-1/2" black and white photograph of a closed casket and floral arrangements. This photograph is marked on the back "Grandma Ray's casket" and also indicates that her photograph hangs on the wall to the left of the casket (it is covered by a floral arrangement). Photograph $25-$30.

Left: The closed casket of "Julius Mueller" taken in a private residence. The floral arrangements indicate "Husband" and "Father." This photograph is another exceptional example of home decorating for the period. Note the piano, wall covering, pictures, carpet, lighting, and accessories. Photograph $40-$50.

The casket of football coach Howard Jones is carried from the First Methodist Church in Hollywood, California. Dated July 31, 1941. *ACME.* Photograph $15-$20.

Original 8" x 10" black and white photograph of the funeral procession for Herbert Straus, executive of a large New York department store. Dated April 9th, 1933. Note the elaborate floral arrangement covering the casket. *ACME.* Photograph $15-$20.

This photograph shows the casket of Benjamin Collings leaving an undertaking parlor in Huntington, Long Island. Dated December 2, 1931. *ACME* Photograph $15-$20.

This copy of a photograph showing a Klu Klux Klan funeral procession in Florida in 1929 was purchased from the eBay auction site. It is shown here for historical reasons and does not reflect any opinion of the seller, buyer, author, or publisher. *Original in Private Collection*. Copy $18-$20.

Pallbearers carry the casket of Ellis H. Parker, Sr., to its final resting place in January, 1940. Parker died in a federal prison where he was serving a sentence for conspiracy to kidnap Paul H. Wendell in an attempt to solve the disappearance of the Lindbergh baby. *ACME*. Photograph $30-$40.

Vaults

A *casket* is an encasement made of either metal, wood, or Grecian marble into which a body is placed. A *vault* is a prefabricated container, usually constructed of metal or concrete, into which the casket is then placed for burial. A vault is often referred to as a "burial chamber" and helps to preserve the body and casket from decay. Vaults are sold either "sealed" or "non-sealed" and it is the choice of the family which one to select. Many families still believe in the old "ashes to ashes, dust to dust" concept, so they purchase a "non-sealed" vault. This is referred to as a "rough-box" or "grave-liner." Vaults are not always required by law, but most states and cemeteries do require a vault.

Postcard showing the Bell Vault & Monument Works, Inc. Miamisburg, Ohio. "This firm was established in 1928. It is now one of the largest combined monument and vault companies in the states. Ten different style Burial Vaults including the nationally known WILBERT BURIAL VAULT. We specialize in GRANITES shipped from most all sections of the world; which are made into Monuments, Markers and Mausoleums of your choice. Over 400 monument and markers on display." $5-$8.

This historical 1920s photograph may have been used as an advertisement for a casket and/or vault company. The vault lid is suspended above the casket by a series of ropes and cables. The casket is supported on the vault's base. *Blackstone Collection.* Photograph $75-100.

58

An employee of a vault company stands among vaults, location unknown. *Neel Collection*. Photograph $100-$150.

The MT. VERNON
12 Gauge
THE CHAMPION COMPANY
SPRINGFIELD, OHIO

The Mt. Vernon 12 Gauge metal vault, made by The Champion Company, Springfield, Ohio. There were (and still are) numerous companies producing vaults across the United States—it is impossible to show advertisements for every make and model of vault that was available. This original advertisement is only a sample of the promotional endorsements from this company. *Private Collection*. Photograph $15-$20.

Salesman sample vaults. *Private Collection.* $45-$50 each.

In 1927, the Clark Grave Vault Company of Columbus, Ohio produced more vaults than in any other location in the world. In the historical photographs shown here (used for advertisement purposes in 1956), Clark Grave Vaults showed no evidence of rust or corrosion after sixteen years of burial (left photograph). The contents (right photograph) were in excellent condition and dry after thirty years of burial and three floods.

Burial Garments

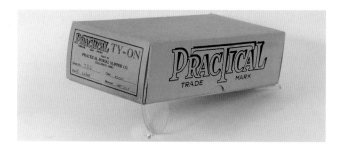

This empty carton contained "Practical™" slippers, made by the Practical Burial Slipper Co., Columbus, Ohio. *S.L. Davis Collection.* $20-$25.

The selection of a burial garment is left to the surviving family members. Clothing may be purchased directly from the undertaker or provided by the family. Vintage burial garments are popular among collectors and have only recently begun to escalate in price. Condition, era, style, and packaging contribute to the selling price.

It is not a common practice today to bury the deceased in their "Sunday best." A wide selection of burial garments are offered or the family may prefer to choose a more casual garment from the private wardrobe. There is no law that presently controls the garments of a deceased, though as a practice the body is fully clothed. Whether jewelry is used as an accessory is left entirely up to the family. Various objects related to the deceased can be buried with them; these include jewelry, books, photographs, religious items, toys, ashes of pets, or any small item of sentimental value related to the deceased.

Bag from Florence Gowns, Inc. Cleveland, Ohio. This bag held burial garments that were delivered to the funeral home. *Ann Davis Collection.* $10-$15.

This "Cincinnati Coffin Co., Cincinnati, Ohio" inspection slip was placed inside burial garments. *S.L. Davis Collection.* $2-$5.

Burial Garments Help Build ....
.... Profits and Prestige

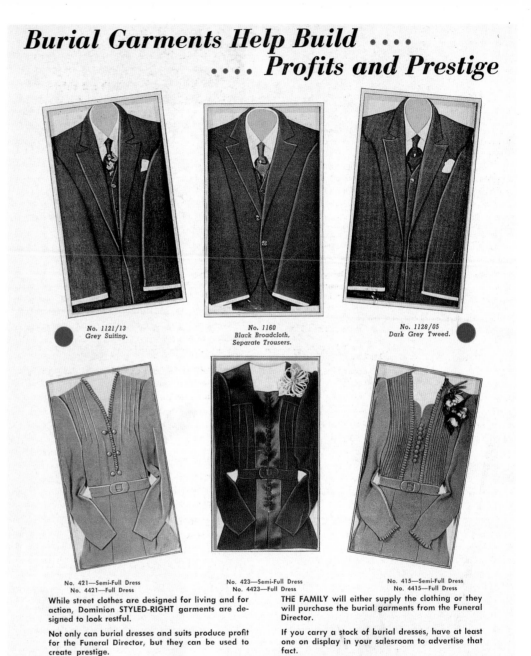

No. 1121/13 Grey Suiting.

No. 1160 Black Broadcloth, Separate Trousers.

No. 1128/05 Dark Grey Tweed.

No. 421—Semi-Full Dress
No. 4421—Full Dress

No. 423—Semi-Full Dress
No. 4423—Full Dress

No. 415—Semi-Full Dress
No. 4415—Full Dress

While street clothes are designed for living and for action, Dominion STYLED-RIGHT garments are designed to look restful.

Not only can burial dresses and suits produce profit for the Funeral Director, but they can be used to create prestige.

THE FAMILY will either supply the clothing or they will purchase the burial garments from the Funeral Director.

If you carry a stock of burial dresses, have at least one on display in your salesroom to advertise that fact.

Dominion offers a large range to choose from, in both Ladies' and Gentlemen's models. Inquire from our salesmen or write Head Office, direct.

In 1942, Dominion offered a large variety of both ladies' and gentlemen's burial garments that were "designed to look restful." The family could either supply the clothing or purchase the burial garments from the funeral director. Prices for vintage burial garments will vary due to geographic locations, condition, packaging, and era.

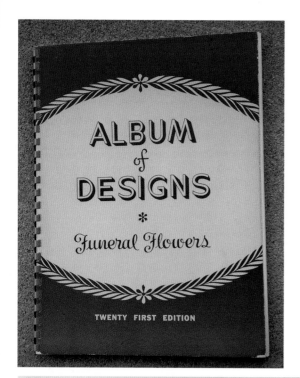

"Album of Designs / Funeral Flowers." Twenty-First Edition, published by Florists' Publishing Co. Publishers of The Florists' Review, Chicago, Illinois. This 95-page catalogue shows funeral arrangements for wreaths, vases, baskets, sprays, and casket covers and includes a page of fraternal emblems. *Blackstone Collection.* $15-$20.

Floral Arrangements

Floral arrangements are sent in remembrance of the deceased to convey the deepest sentiment. Each arrangement was properly placed around the casket with consideration of color and visual effect. Floral arrangements achieve the proper effect when displayed on white, wrought-iron stands. Sympathy offerings in large handled baskets were often used for easy handling. Vases and basket designs often gave an arrangement the proper dignity; they were, and still are, the most popular sympathy offerings.

Taken in front of a Menominee, Michigan church in 1930, this snapshot shows an example of "flowergirls," often older women who attended to the removal of floral arrangements after a funeral service. Each woman in the photo is holding a floral offering as pallbearers carry the casket to be interred in the church cemetery. This once popular procedure is no longer used. In some parts of the United States, however, it is still popular today for a member of the family to hold a basket of cut flowers to pass out after the committal service at the grave site. Mourners then place the flowers on top of the casket upon leaving the service. Some families order special floral offerings to have on hand for the day of the service. Others remove flowers from those baskets available at the grave site. Originally the tradition of sending floral offerings was to cover up the odor of the body. *Blackstone Collection.* Photograph $10-15.

Left: Floral arrangements were photographed in this private residence. Vintage wicker funeral baskets are highly sought by collectors. These baskets will vary in price range. *Blackstone Collection.* Photograph $15-$20.

This photograph of floral arrangements was taken by Orr-Kiefer in a Columbus, Ohio private residence. *Blackstone Collection.* Photograph $15-$20.

IN MEMORY OF A MOTHER

"I remember thee in this solemn hour, my dear mother. I remember the days when thou didst dwell on earth, and thy tender love watched over me like a guardian angel. Thou had gone from me, but the bond which unite our souls can never be severed; thine image lives within my heart. May the merciful Father reward thee for the faithfulness and kindness thou hast ever shown me; may He lift up the light of his countenance upon thee and grant thee eternal peace! Amen."

An example of proper placement of floral and casket arrangement, taken in Edwardsville, Illinois. The casket arrangement indicates "MOTHER." *Blackstone Collection.* Photograph $35-$40.

Public Viewing

This photograph is dated 1936 and indicates on the back that it shows "Police Commissioner Heinrich Pickert" viewing a senator who is lying in state. *Central Press Association*. Photograph $15-$20.

Parents pay final tribute to their daughter. This photograph is dated June 3, 1938. *Central Press Association*. Photograph $15-$20.

This photograph showing an Asian American public viewing and funeral was taken in California. *McGuire Collection*. Photograph $45-$50.

Salvation Army funeral viewing. *Blackstone Collection*. Photograph $50-$60.

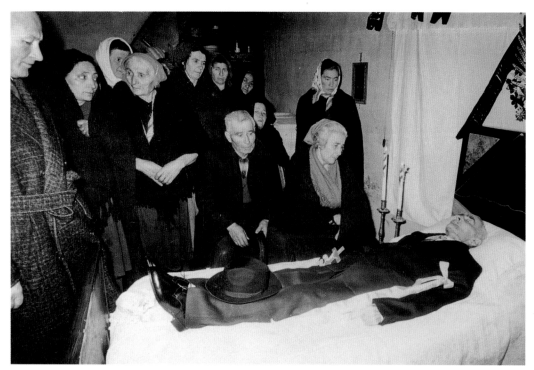

In this photograph taken in Southern Italy, a family pays their final respects to a deceased member, laid out on a bed. Note the hat resting on his legs. *Courtesy of Daniel W. Pallay, Director, Cook & Son, Pallay Funeral Home.* NFS.

Public viewing of deceased. *Courtesy of Daniel W. Pallay, Director, Cook & Son, Pallay Funeral Home.* NFS.

Funeral service. *Courtesy of Daniel W. Pallay, Director, Cook & Son, Pallay Funeral Home.* NFS.

Funeral procession. *Courtesy of Daniel W. Pallay, Director, Cook & Son, Pallay Funeral Home.* NFS.

Part 4
Cremation and Burial

Cremation chamber or retort room. This chamber was installed during the 1940s.

Cremation

One form of disposition of the deceased is through the process of cremation: the body, which has been enclosed in a combustible container such as wood or cardboard and then subjected to intense heat, is diminished to skeletal fragments in ash form in less than 2-1/2 to 3 hours.

The procedure is done in a cremation retort chamber that cremates the body at a temperature of 1600-1800 degrees Fahrenheit. In describing a cremated body the shortened word version is "cremains," also meaning "cremated remains." The cremains of an average size adult weigh between three and nine pounds.

The disposition of a body through cremation is only a process and not a replacement for the more traditional funeral to which we are accustomed. Today, an increasing number of people are selecting cremation over earth burial because of the cost factor, simplicity, and environmental concerns. It is estimated that the cost of cremation is approximately 20% lower than earth burial.

Public viewing and honoring of the deceased with the body present, along with a funeral service, provide comfort to the family members and friends who are mourning. For a public viewing the body is embalmed; if a body is to be cremated upon death, most states do not require embalming. Services also can be held after cremation with the cremated remains present in a temporary or permanent urn. The location of the service can be a private home, place of worship, crematory, or just prior to the grave site burial of the urn in a cemetery plot, above ground mausoleum, or columbarium. A scattering service, in which the ashes are scattered over an open area of sentiment value, is another option. Only those areas permitted by law should be chosen. Many times an urn containing the ashes of a loved one has been kept in the home and passed down generation to generation. This procedure is still practiced today.

Metal caskets are not allowed or convenient for cremation. Many funeral homes, however, offer a standard metal casket which has a lining insert where the body is in repose. After the services, the insert and deceased are removed as one unit and the process of cremation is begun. A new insert is then placed inside the casket, which is used again. This procedure has only been recently implemented within the past few years.

This 16-page booklet was available from "The Cincinnati Cremation Company" to anyone interested in learning more about cremation. The "Crematory" was erected in 1887 on Dixmyth Avenue to address the growing demands of the city's population, the need for reduced cost of funerals, and protection of the remains from the disrespectful treatment that often befalls graves in city burial grounds. The Columbarium (a vault with niches for urns containing the ashes of cremated bodies) was designed by Cincinnati architect Gustave W. Drach of bronzed iron. *Chapman Collection*. $40-$50.

In 1936, cremation was not a customary method of disposal. The funeral director's sole desire, during that era, was to serve the family and its wishes. A director held no brief for or against this procedure and if cremation was requested arrangements for this were made.

Cremation casket.

Earth Burial

Interred in a single Lot Number 1302 of Section 34 in Green Lawn Cemetery, Columbus, Ohio (shown above) is William H. Wise, born July 11, 1870 in Columbus and died June 30, 1890 in Columbus. The son of Wilson and Sarah Wise, William's cause of death is recorded in the Green Lawn Cemetery office as "Struck By Lightning." Interred July 2, 1890 and listed in card file record as No. 16901. His grave site could not be located.

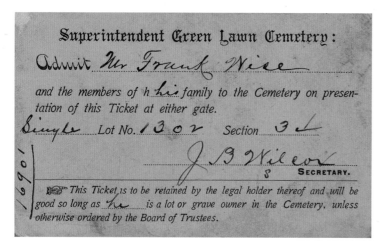

This Green Lawn Cemetery pass "No. 16901" permitted the family of William H. Wise entrance at either gate upon presentation of this ticket. Rules and Regulations were indicated on the reserve side of the pass and were to be observed by "Lot-holders and Visitors." *Private Collection.* $30-$40.

Earth burial is the most common form of interment. The opening of a grave site is approximately 4' x 8' and the average cost of an adult funeral in the United States in 1998 was approximately $5,020 to $5,988, which includes an average of $2,176 for the casket.

A large percentage of the population believes that digging a hole and burying $5,000 to $10,000 in it is unprecedented; there are others, however, who still believe in traditional funerals and are willing to pay $8,000 to $11,000 to have one. Everyone has his or her own viewpoint on this subject.

Discount funerals are beginning to become popular in major cities.

This is a copy of an original 1940s photograph of "Grave-Diggers" which is presently in the collection of the Green Lawn Cemetery, Columbus, Ohio. Green Lawn Cemetery was founded August 2, 1848. *Photograph courtesy Green Lawn Cemetery.*

Bereavement of family and friends are shown in the burial photograph above, location unknown. *Neill Collection.* Photograph $15-$20.

"Jesus said suffer the little children to come unto me, for such is the kingdom of heaven." Dated 1930, burial of a child in Michigan. *ACME.* Photograph $30-$40.

Burial in a church cemetery, location and date unknown. Photograph $15-$20.

Burial of a loved one in St. Jerome, Canada. *Neill Collection.* Photograph $45-$50.

A grieving widow, family and friends at the grave site of a loved one. *Blackstone Collection.* Photograph $5-$10.

Family and friends prepare to leave the grave site of a loved one, location unknown. *Blackstone Collection.* Photograph $15-$20.

In this 1950s burial photograph taken in California, a large gathering of family and friends pays its final respects. *Blackstone Collection.* Photograph $75-$100.

Family and friends gather at an Akron, Ohio grave site. Note the window in the lid of this coffin, which rests upon a wheelbarrow. The handles can be seen directly under the coffin. *Blackstone Collection.* Photograph $125-$150.

74

Mausoleums

"In the garden of memories we meet every day, I miss you more and more. In life I loved you dearly, In death I love you still, in my heart you hold a place no one can ever fill." ©*Wendell & Co. Memorial Flyer, 1900.*

Private and public mausoleums date back to ancient times and are resonant with rich history. They represent a classic tale of love and the revelation of tender devotion from one to another at the time of death. In form, they are magnificent monuments of marble, bronze, and stained glass, built for ages.

The advantages of entombment in a mausoleum were: the assurance of perpetual care and maintenance; low cost; exclusiveness; and, for many, the comfort that loved ones were interred in dry crypts with their names perpetuated for centuries in magnificent stone.

This magnificent mausoleum known as the "Green Lawn Abbey" opened in 1927 at the intersection of Harmon Road and Green Lawn Avenue in Columbus, Ohio. Little history of the actual construction is known or can be located, as the records are incomplete. I have been told that a prominent Columbus resident wanted an elaborate private memorial built for himself and capitalized on the idea that if other people were buried there he could build it on an ancient Greco-Roman grandeur scale. When he died, he left no provisions in his will for perpetual care and over the years the building gradually began to decay. Others believe that a group of prominent Columbus residents are responsible for the building of this magnificent structure. I have not been able to confirm either of these stories, but continue to do research. If readers have any knowledge, records, or family members buried in this mausoleum, please contact me through the publisher. Note that there is no connection between the "Green Lawn Abbey" and the "Green Lawn Cemetery."

The "Abbey" is a magnificent monument to the more than 440 people entombed. It is constructed in a classical design of marble and bronze, and has numerous stained glassed windows throughout the two floors. The upper level has the most elaborate crypts, with as many as ten crypts per room secured by locked bronze gates. It is estimated that in 1929 a crypt for four cost $2,500.

Some of the most prominent Columbus residents rest within the foot and a half thick walls of the Green Lawn Abbey: Sells brothers traveling circus founder Lewis Sells; housing developer Charles Foster Johnson; two-time Columbus mayor and former county sheriff, George J. Karb; and Dr. Charles J. and Mabel Holbrook Shepard. (Dr. Shepard was the first dermatologist in the city and one of the founders of the Ohio State University Medical School of Dermatology. He was a student of Dr. Max Joseph in Germany.) Howard Thurston, the famous magician and illusionist, was also buried there in 1936. Many of those wealthy enough commissioned the construction of their own religious statuary, which are placed behind locked gates. Pieces of statuary that stand along the interior hallways have been damaged by a thief(s) in the night, as shown here. Presently, an organization is being developed to preserve this mausoleum and its grounds.

Barrick Mausoleum, West Lawn Cemetery, Canton, Ohio. *Courtesy of Cindy L. Donovan.*

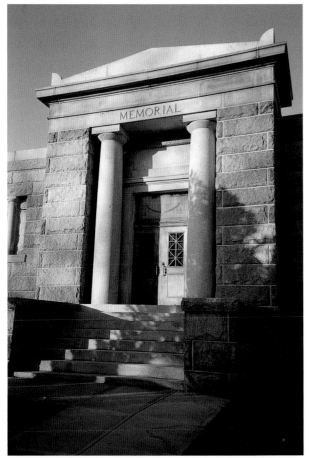

Greenwood Cemetery Mausoleum, Zanesville, Ohio. The entrance to this cemetery can be seen on the postcard shown on page 137. *Courtesy of Rod Blackstone.*

Hasler Mausoleum 1908, West Lawn Cemetery, Canton, Ohio. *Courtesy of Cindy L. Donovan.*

Renkert Mausoleum, West Lawn Cemetery, Canton, Ohio. *Courtesy of Cindy L. Donovan.*

Entrance to President William McKinley Monument and Mausoleum, West Lawn Cemetery, Canton, Ohio. *Courtesy of Cindy L. Donovan.*

This "Receiving Vault," built in 1893, was the temporary resting place for President William McKinley from September 19, 1901 until completion of the McKinley National Memorial in West Lawn Cemetery. Mrs. Ida McKinley came to this site daily until her death in 1907, when she was entombed in the receiving vault along with her husband. In September 1907, Mr. and Mrs. McKinley and their two young daughters were moved to the McKinley National Memorial. (For those interested, West Lawn Cemetery provides a Historic Walking Tour from May 1 through October 31, which begins through the cemetery gates on 7th Street N.W. The gates are open from 8 a.m. until 7 p.m. weekdays and from 10 a.m. until 7 p.m. Sundays and holidays. The cemetery closes at 5 p.m. during the winter months.) *Courtesy of Cindy L. Donovan.*

"Charles H. Hayden" mausoleum, Green Lawn Cemetery, Columbus, Ohio. Twelve members of the prominent C.H. Hayden family of Columbus are buried in the "Hayden" family mausoleum. Each member is buried in a separate vault located within the majestic mausoleum. Family members include: son, Harry Hayden, born October 2, 1877 and died July 10, 1878 (his body was moved into the mausoleum in 1907); daughter, Florence L. Hayden, born March 27, 1858 and died October 17, 1881 (her body was moved into the mausoleum in 1907); daughter, Daisy Hayden Bonsol (records show her last name spelled Bonsal), born April 7, 1877 and died February 19, 1895 (her body was moved into the mausoleum in 1907); son, Peter Hallock Hayden (his body was moved from New Jersey to the family mausoleum December 6, 1907); and daughter, Edith E. Hayden, May 18, 1909; Charles H. Hayden, August 27, 1920, and his wife Louise Irving Hayden, December 12, 1910; grandson, Charles Hayden Bonsal, May 6, 1926; daughter, Lillian Hayden Fenton, May 9, 1933; daughter, Bellie Hayden Prentiss, February 16, 1939; daughter Marie Hayden Powell, February 28, 1979; and the cremated ashes of son, Charles Everett Hayden, 1940. *Courtesy of Rod Blackstone.*

Late afternoon sun illuminates the weathered entrance to the "Charles H. Hayden" mausoleum in Green Lawn Cemetery, Columbus, Ohio. Two sets of secured doors open into the main chamber: iron gates measuring approximately 11' 8-1/4" by 6' 5-1/4", slide into the exterior walls; the second set is of solid wood. Presently the iron gates have been secured by a heavy chain and lock. *Courtesy of Rod Blackstone.*

"Gay" mausoleum in Green Lawn Cemetery, Columbus, Ohio. Interred here are Harvey D. Gay, son of Merrick and Sarah Gay, born December 19, 1829 in Georgesville, Vermont, died July 24, 1878; and Virginia Walcott Gay, daughter of John M. and Muriel Broderick Walcutt, born May 9, 1831 in Columbus, Ohio, died May 8, 1914. *Courtesy of Rod Blackstone*.

"Evans" mausoleum in Green Lawn Cemetery, Columbus, Ohio. Interred here are Charles Frazer Evans, 1856-1939; Mary Hopkins Evans, 1858-1940; Charles Hopkins Evans, 1880-1901; Nelson Frazer Evans, 1889-1922; and Clara Hopkins Scott, 1848-1926. *Courtesy of Rod Blackstone*.

Fredericka Gutheil, 1835-1916, mausoleum in Green Lawn Cemetery, Columbus, Ohio. *Courtesy of Rod Blackstone*.

John Beals Brown, January 8, 1864-August 10, 1931, mausoleum in Green Lawn Cemetery, Columbus, Ohio. *Courtesy of Rod Blackstone.*

Three examples of the many private mausoleums on Green Lawn Cemetery grounds: "John Gordon Battelle," "Horace J. Maynard - J. Elwood Bulen," and "Packard" mausoleums. Fresh flowers are still delivered weekly to the Battelle mausoleum. *Courtesy of Rod Blackstone.*

"Howald" mausoleum. This mausoleum overlooks the original stone quarry. In use from the late 1800s to the 1920s, stones from this quarry were used to lay the base of the cemetery roads. The pond or pit, as it is often referred to, is kept in its natural state for use and preservation of the wildlife. The water is from an underground aquifer. *Courtesy of Rod Blackstone.*

Monuments

This late 1920s historical photograph shows the Thomas and Bowker Memorials Company in Bordentown, New Jersey. *Courtesy of Rod Blackstone.* Photograph $40-$50.

The soaring obelisks and majestic architectural monuments of cemeteries beckon visitors to venture into these cities of the dead. Roaming among the monuments of marble and cast bronze, one feels their elegance, strength, stability, sincerity, distinctiveness, and dignity. From the opulent to the indigent, we can glean vast amounts of historical information from the epitaphs and prominent names chiseled into the stone. In these acres we have immortalized the sentiment and reverence of the community.

Many monuments are cut with various symbols, images, and motifs representing "Life, Death, and Burial." Laurel leaves, a Roman sword, a butterfly, and a snake symbol represent "Resurrection." An hourglass, scythe, and pair of wings represent "Brief duration of life on Earth." "Sorrow" is often indicated with the willow branch, "Trinity, Faith, Odd Fellows" by a chain with three links. "Farewell, hope of meeting in eternity" is represented by clasped hands. Burial symbols are numerous and this represents only a sample listing.

Numerous catalogues, booklets, and advertisements related to monuments, granite, and marble works are available to collectors. In 1946, for example, a thirty-six page color publication called *Heritage™ Memorials* was available upon request from Sears, Roebuck and Co. Sears "Heritage™ Memorials" could be delivered and erected anywhere in the United States (photograph of this publication not available).

The monument of Ann Davis, died June 5, 1851 aged 86 years 5 months 8 days and her husband John Davis died January 25, 1832 aged 71 years 4 month 19 days. "Ann Davis was messenger and carried orders from General Washington to the other commanders in the Revolutionary war in 1779-1780." "John Davis was a soldier in the Revolutionary war and served from 1777 to 1781 in the Pennsylvania Reg'ts." These inscriptions appear on the side of their monument located in the "Davis Historical Cemetery," Dublin, Ohio.

This historical photograph of the "SINCLAIR" monument, Juliann Sinclair 1830-1880 and Thomas Sinclair 1832-1902 was taken in Pennsylvania. *Neel Collection.* Photograph $25-$35.

This grave site photograph was taken in Pennsylvania. Note the lone chair on the right and the gentleman kneeling at the grave site to the left. The recumbent lamb marks that of a infant grave. Children were often memorialized with tiny lambs or broken pillars, indicating a life cut short. *Neel Collection.* Photograph $35-$45.

Epitaphs

Forty-nine epitaphs have been gathered for this publication. I appreciate those who so kindly supplied the following (see "Acknowledgments").

"Our loved one."

"Of such is the kingdom of heaven."

"Suffer little children to come unto me."

"In heaven there is one angel more."

"Another little angel. Before the heavenly throne."

"A little time on earth he spent, Till God for him His angel sent."

"A little bud of love. To Bloom with God above."

"Sleep on, sweet babe, and take thy rest. God called thee home, he thought it best."

"Weep not, father and mother, for me. For I am waiting in glory for thee."

"A little flower of love. That blossomed but to die; Transplanted now above, To bloom with God on high."

"At rest."

"We will meet again."

"Gone, but not forgotten."

"Tho' lost to sight, to memory dear."

"Asleep in Jesus."

"His memory is blessed."

"He is not dead, but sleepeth."

"She was the sunshine of our home."

"Resting in hope of a glorious resurrection."

"How desolate our home, bereft of thee."

"He died as he lived—a Christian."

"An honest man's the noblest work of God."

"A tender mother and a faithful friend."

"Faithful to her trust."

"Even unto death."

"Gone to a bright home, Where grief can not come."

"She was a kind and affectionate wife, a fond mother, and a friend to all."

"Rest, mother, rest in quiet sleep, While friends in sorrow o'er thee weep."

"God gave, He took, He will restore, He doeth all things well."

"To him, we trust, a place is given, Among the saints with Christ in heaven."

"Having finished life's duty, She now sweetly rests."

"His toils are part, his work is done. He fought the fight—the victory won."

"May the resurrection find thee, On the bosom of thy God."

"None knew thee but to love thee, None named thee but to praise."

"Just in the morning of his day, In youth and love, he died."

"The sweet remembrances of the just. Shall flourish when they sleep in dust."

"Dearest brother, thou hast left us. Here, thy loss we deeply feel. But 'tis God that hath bereft us, He can all our sorrows heal."

"Although he sleeps. His memory doth live. And cheering comfort, To his mourners give."

"Calm on the bosom of thy God, Young Spirit, rest thee now, E'en while with us thy footsteps trod, His seal was on thy brow."

"She hath done what she could."

"There shall be no night there."

"Be thou faithful unto death, and I will give thee a crown of life."

"Blessed are the pure in heart; for they shall see God."

"I have fought a good fight, I have finished my course, I have kept the faith."

"I know that my Redeemer liveth."

"I am the resurrection and the life."

"A friend to his country and a believer in Christ."

"Nobly he fell while fighting for liberty."

"Behold and see as you pass by. As you are now, so once was I. As I am now, so you must be. Prepare for death and follow me."

The Tablet

The "tablet" monument, a slab-form with or without a base, is the most prevalent of all monuments in many cemeteries. This monument may be either horizontal or vertical in form.

The "CARPENTER" monument located in Green Lawn Cemetery, Columbus, Ohio. *Courtesy Carolyn McGuire.*

The "SNYDER" monument located in Green Lawn Cemetery, Columbus, Ohio. *Courtesy Carolyn McGuire.*

The "Cross" and "Cross Tablet"

Of all the memorials for the Christian cemetery, the "Cross" and "Cross Tablet" were the most significant. The most favored monuments were the Celtic, the Gothic, and the Latin. The "Cross Tablet" is believed to have its origin in the erect Cross slabs of Christian Celtic times, which feature the Cross carved in relief on an upright slab.

Damage has occurred to this "Cross" monument located in Green Lawn Cemetery, Columbus, Ohio. Many cemeteries are subject to desecration by vandalism. *Courtesy Carolyn McGuire.*

"SISTERS OF THE HOLY CROSS," Mt. Calvary Cemetery, Columbus, Ohio. *Courtesy Rod Blackstone.*

"IN MEMORY OF SISTER MAGDALEN OF ST. BERNADINE," Mt. Calvary Cemetery, Columbus, Ohio. *Courtesy Rod Blackstone.*

This "Cross" has a carved relief on the upright slab. Mt. Calvary Cemetery, Columbus, Ohio. *Courtesy Rod Blackstone.*

The Sarcophagus

In ancient Egypt, Greece, and Rome, the sarcophagus was used for actual entombment. During the nineteenth century, the sarcophagus was a favorite, soon becoming merely a family memorial. Some sarcophagi accommodate two interments.

Opposite page: "Frederick Schumacher" metal sarcophagus in Green Lawn Cemetery, Columbus, Ohio, one of the most popular and photographed of all grave sites in this historical cemetery. Schumacher married into the prominent "Dr. Samuel Brubaker Hartman" family of Columbus. Dr. Hartman created the famous patent medicine called "Peruna," which contained a large amount of liquor but maintained its famous claim as medicine. Schumacher later divorced his wife and is buried alone in this magnificent sarcophagus. *Courtesy Rod Blackstone.*

"Bishop Watterson" sarcophagus in Mt. Calvary Cemetery, Columbus, Ohio. *Courtesy Rod Blackstone.*

An example of the "PALMER" exedra, in Green Lawn Cemetery, Columbus, Ohio. *Courtesy Rod Blackstone.*

The Exedra

An exedra is often referred to as a monumental seat. It is usually elliptical or semi-circular. Modern exedrae can range from the simple garden bench set against a wall or screen, to the impressive architectural shape. These monuments were usually located at the rear of the plot.

Beautiful example of the "HOSTER" exedra, in Green Lawn Cemetery, Columbus, Ohio. The Hoster family were affluent in the Columbus area. *Courtesy Rod Blackstone.*

The Columnar Monument

The "columnar monument" has appealed to mankind since the ancient Greeks perfected this element in architectural design. This monument may be a single column or may surmount a pedestal or steps.

An example of a pedestal columnar monument in Green Lawn Cemetery, Columbus, Ohio. *Courtesy Rod Blackstone.*

This is a beautiful example of a columnar monument which surrounds a pedestal sculpture bust under an ornamental canopy. This example illustrates excellent architectural design combining the columns, sculpture, canopy, and base. Green Lawn Cemetery, Columbus, Ohio. *Courtesy Rod Blackstone.*

The "MOON" and "LANG" columnar monument, Green Lawn Cemetery, Columbus, Ohio. *Courtesy Rod Blackstone.*

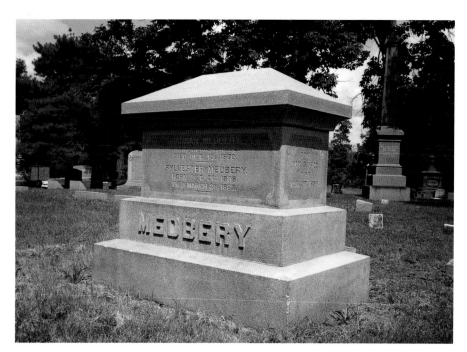

Example of multiple monument in Green Lawn Cemetery for "MEDBERY," "STEDMAN," and "TUTTLE." Hannah Medbery 1802-1870, Lucy Stedman 1820-1898, Sylvester 1808-1887, and Catharine Tuttle 1823-1910. *Courtesy Rod Blackstone.*

Example of square sided monument for "HOOPES." Thomas Hoopes was the founder of Hoopeston, Illinois. In 1854, Hoopes arrived in Vermilion County, Illinois and established his grand home on a section of his 480 acres of land north of the present city of Hoopeston. He continued to purchase land and by the time the railroad arrived, Hoopes owned approximately 7,000 acres of rich and fertile farm land. He visualized the possibility of establishing a city at the intersections of the Nickel Plate Railroad and the Chicago & Eastern Illinois Railroad, which crossed his land, and thus began laying off a portion of his farm land into city lots. Floral Hill Cemetery, Hoopeston, Illinois. *Courtesy Karen and Sadie Evans.*

The Pedestal and Square Monument

The pedestal and square monument allows three or more families equally important sides for the family name. This monument was also popular for single families. They were once referred to as "Cottage Monuments," which soon became obsolete.

"SULLIVANT" square sided monument. Green Lawn Cemetery, Columbus, Ohio. *Courtesy Rod Blackstone.*

A majestic example of a pedestal monument in Green Lawn Cemetery, Columbus, Ohio. Some students of history also refer to this monument as an "Obelisk." *Courtesy Rod Blackstone.*

Placement of an "Obelisk" is shown in this historical postcard. *Courtesy Rod Blackstone*. Postcard $75-$100.

The Obelisk

The obelisk is the grandest of all monuments. Obelisks are most effective when their height exceeds twenty-five feet elevation.

Example of an "Obelisk" in Elgin, Illinois in 1887. *Courtesy Rod Blackstone*. Postcard $50-$60.

Beautiful example of an "Obelisk," Green Lawn Cemetery, Columbus, Ohio. *Courtesy Rod Blackstone*.

The Sculptured Memorial

Once lacking in this country were sculptured monuments. During the mid-1800s, however, sculptors began collaborating with monument designers and cemetery officials in an effort to bring to America the sculptured shrines of art form like those abroad. Today we see various forms of statuary throughout many of our cemeteries, from those sculptured of marble to those of majestic bronze.

An example of sculptured beauty. Bonaventure Cemetery, Savannah, Georgia.

This life-size sculpture in Green Lawn Cemetery, Columbus, Ohio is that of George Blount. George was killed when he fell over a banister at the American House Hotel and died on Valentine's Day in 1873 at the age of five. He was the son of E.J. and S.A. Blount. As the seasons pass, so does his attire. An unknown person or persons continues to clothe the statue of George in seasonal attire and also buys him presents. In this photograph he wears an O.S.U. cap and is holding flowers. George is never forgotten. *Courtesy Rod Blackstone.*

This majestic monument was "Erected By The Franklin County Ex-Soldiers and Sailors Association And The County Commissioners," 1890. Green Lawn Cemetery has six sections that are specified for the burial of veterans: Section "M" Civil War, Section "28" Soldier & Sailors, Section "51" Spanish American, Section "71" World War I, Section "104" World War II, and Section "105," which opened in 1987. *Courtesy Rod Blackstone.*

Located in Green Lawn Cemetery, Columbus, Ohio, this is the final resting place of Eliza G. Sullivant, wife of William S. Sullivant and daughter of Eliphalet & Mary M. Wheeler. Born in the City of New York. March 11, 1817. Died in Ohio, August 23, 1850. Her head and shoulders are sculpted into her monument, set among a garland of *Sullivantia sullivantii.*

This beautiful statue is located in Mt. Calvary Cemetery, Columbus, Ohio. *Courtesy Rod Blackstone.*

Memorials of the Garden Type

Memorial art combined with proper landscaping can transform the cemetery into a garden of memory. Numerous monument craftsmen have adapted architectural garden art into cemetery memorials. These include the sun-dial, garden bench, pergola, garden urn, and even bird baths, for many of our cemeteries are bird sanctuaries.

This iron garden bench sits behind a monument in Christ Union Cemetery, Trumbauersville, Bucks County, Pennsylvania. *Courtesy Joan Neel.*

Garden bench monument in Green Lawn Cemetery, Columbus, Ohio. *Courtesy Rod Blackstone.*

Interred in a Quebec, Canada cemetery is "Sumner Everett - Died March 25th, 1891, aged 1 year 15 days." Note the ornate iron fence surrounding his grave and the name plate on the front gate reading "J.C. EVERETT." Ornate iron work such as this was popular during the 1800s - late 1900s. *Private Collection.* Photograph $25-35.

These beautiful urns stand at the entrance to a family grave site in Green Lawn Cemetery, Columbus, Ohio. *Courtesy Rod Blackstone*.

Cemeteries attract both wildlife and human interests. Gene Stauffer of Grove City, Ohio often comes to Green Lawn Cemetery to watch for birds. *Courtesy Gene Stauffer*.

An example of a garden urn. *Courtesy Rod Blackstone*.

The Screen

Similar in design to the exedra, but without a seat, a "screen" is wall-like in form and located at the rear of the plot. A balustrade was often incorporated into the design.

Beautiful example of the "JEFFREY" family screen monument in Green Lawn Cemetery. *Courtesy Rod Blackstone.*

The "HOSTER" family screen monument. Many of those who contributed to the history of Columbus, Ohio came to rest at Green Lawn Cemetery. *Courtesy Rod Blackstone.*

The Mission of Beauty in The Cemetery

"Not until sorrow comes to us can we fully appreciate the function of beauty and sentiment in relieving our desolation and despair. Just as the architectural glory of an impressive church or temple can lift the spirit of man, so likewise the tranquility of a beautiful cemetery can lighten the burden of sorrow. More than that, the prevalence of beauty and sentiment in the cemetery inspires a nobler and a healthier attitude toward the great transition. Truly therefore it may be said that the beautification of the cemetery is an obligation to the living no less than a tribute to the dead." *Memorial Extension Commission, Inc. ©1934.*

This monument is not discussed above or classified. I received this impressive photograph of individual interment from a special friend who has recently taken an interest in her family genealogy, monuments, and the preservation of cemeteries. These monuments are located in Christ Union Cemetery, Trumbauersville, Bucks County, Pennsylvania. *Courtesy Joan Neel.*

Part 5
Postmortem

It often is a shock to realize that some people merely shudder when death is discussed. In this "Pulaski, Va." photograph, a family mourns the passing of a loved one by having a group photograph taken. This procedure was not uncommon during the 1900s. A framed photograph of the deceased, to the right, is draped in black, three members are dressed in mourning black, one is dressed in printed material, and the gentleman is attired in a dark suit. It is believed this group is the brother and sisters of the deceased. *Neel Collection.* Photograph $75-$80.

Some difficult decisions needed to be made when selecting photographs for the following section. I had acquired more than eight hundred original postmortem photographs to select from (this figure does not include those photographs that appear elsewhere in this publication). It was impossible, however, to reproduce every postmortem photograph that had been lent to me from private collections as well as those from my own collection.

After carefully studying each photograph, eliminations were made and photographs were selected based upon subject matter, architectural surrounds, clarity, era, rarity, interior design, condition, and uniqueness.

Names, dates, and location are provided in the caption if the original photograph identified them. It was not uncommon for family members to provide information on the reverse side of old photographs indicating the name of the deceased, date of death, and sometimes their birth. Many photographs, however, provided no information.

Collectors may have difficulty locating the specific photographs shown in this section because of the limited number of copies produced for a bereaved family. Many of the collectors who provided postmortem photographs are known in this area to trade, swap, and sell among other collectors, due to of the limited subject matter or the desire to have such a photograph. This section is meant to illustrate the characteristics and broad array of postmortem photographs available. This can become a very expensive hobby as prices vary depending on geographical locations.

As noted in an earlier section, the term "whole couch" refers to a casket that has a lid open the full length of the casket. The term "half couch" is used to describe a casket with a lid open showing just the upper half.

The thin veil fabric or netting draped across the opening of the casket is referred to as an "illusion veil." This veil was popular at one time when people were laid out in their homes, often to keep inquisitive people and flies away from the casket. Before embalming became an art, the veil was often placed across the opening for those bodies that did not look so exceptional. The veil is often used today in cases of accident victims, so the family can still identify the person, but not see how poorly he or she looks.

Many of the following postmortem photographs lack information or any identification. In memory of those shown in this section I am providing the most popular and/or appropriate epitaph as their only caption. A partial listing of "Epitaphs" appears on page 85.

This photograph was taken in Brazil, Indiana. Flowers indicate that she was a "Sister" and "Daughter" and that her name was "Mary." *Neel Collection.* Photograph $75-$80.

"God gave, He took, He will restore, He doeth all things well." *Neel Collection.* Photograph $75-$80.

Unusual example of the deceased reposed on a casket insert. The insert and body were then placed inside casket. *Blackstone Collection.* Photograph $175-$200.

"We will meet again." *Donovan Collection.* Photograph $40-$50.

"Asleep in Jesus." *Donovan Collection*. Photograph $40-$50.

"At Rest." *Alcosiba Collection*. Photograph $90-$100.

Mary Dutko Baranek, born February 2, 1875 in Austria and died January 1931. Buried in Ramey, Pennsylvania cemetery. "Whole Couch" open lid, cloth covered casket with metal handles. Luxurious pleated and heavy draped lining interior. Note torchiere at the foot of the casket and the candelabra. *Courtesy Loretta Baranek Busko*. NFS.

103

"Faithful to her trust, Even unto death." *Alcosiba Collection*. Photograph $80-$90.

"Blessed are the pure in heart; for they shall see God." *Lohrman Collection*. Photograph $40-$50.

"Mother." *Lohrman Collection*. Photograph $100-$125.

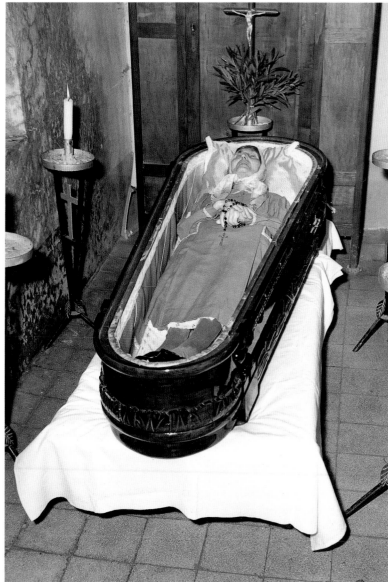

Elegant "Whole Couch" with drop panel side, cloth covered with metal hardware. Interior is heavily lined, pleated and tufted with elaborate draping, and has a floral garland inside lid. Elegant burial garment and floral arrangements with ribbons that drape each end of the drop panel. This photograph provides an excellent pictorial of interior decor at the turn of the twentieth century. Note large family photographs and home furnishings. *Blackstone Collection.* Photograph $175-$200.

"Mother." This photograph was purchased at a tag sale in Columbus, Ohio. Photograph $40-$50.

106

"At Rest." *Frisby Collection*. Photograph
$75-$100.

"Gone, but not forgotten." *Frisby Collection*.
Photograph $75-$100.

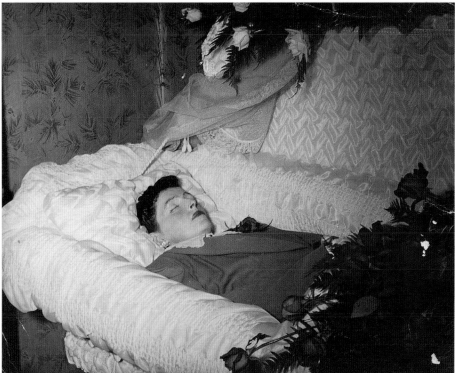

"Having finished life's duty, She now sweetly
rests." *Frisby Collection*. Photograph $100-$125.

107

"Wife and Grandma." *Garrison Collection*. Photograph $75-$100.

"Mother." Richmond, Indiana. *Garrison Collection*. Photograph $75-$100.

"Rest, mother, rest in quiet sleep, While friends in sorrow o'er thee weep." *Garrison Collection*. Photograph $75-$100.

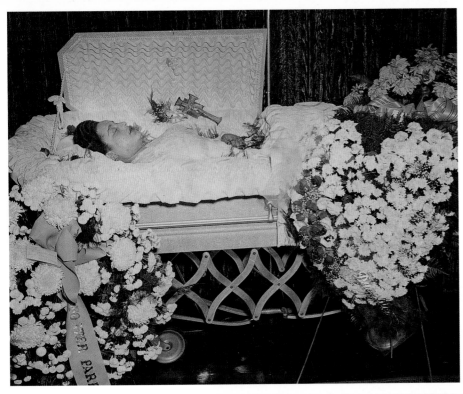

"There shall be no night there." Richmond, Virginia, dated October 1, 1947. *Garrison Collection*. Photograph $75-$100.

"She was the sunshine of our home," "JOSEPHINE." *Private Collection*. Photograph $75-$100.

"At Peace." Zumbrota, Minnesota. *Private Collection*. Photograph $75-$100.

109

"A tender mother and a faithful friend." *Private Collection*. Photograph $75-$100.

"At Peace In Jesus." Port Chester, New York. *Private Collection*. Photograph $75-$100.

"Our loved one." *McGuire Collection*. Photograph $75-$100.

"Her memory is blessed." *McGuire Collection.* Photograph $75-$100.

This photograph is hand-colored, a process that was popular during the 1940s-1960s. Back is inscribed "JO ELLE." *Private Collection.* Photograph $75-$100.

"Lillie Sollars Miller 1883-1955." Hoopeston, Illinois, burial Floral Hill Cemetery. My grandmother. NFS.

Excellent example of burial garment with bonnet and rosary. Photograph is dated
December 24, 1913. *Private Collection*. Photograph $200-$225.

Excellent example of a "Whole Couch" casket, with window lid removed and placed against back wall. *Blackstone Collection.* Photograph $175-$200.

"Gone to a bright home, Where grief can not come." Excellent example of interior home view. *Blackstone Collection.* Photograph $85-$100.

"At Rest." *Blackstone Collection.* Photograph $85-$100.

"At Peace." Circleville, Ohio. *Blackstone Collection.* Photograph $85-$100.

"She is not dead, but sleepeth." *Blackstone Collection.*
Photograph $100-$125.

Beautiful interior view of funeral for "Sister and Aunt," dated July 14, 1925.
Chicago, Illinois. *Private Collection*. Photograph $150-$175.

Family members pose with floral arrangements and the casket of their mother. *Blackstone Collection.* Photograph $75-$100.

"She was the sunshine of our home." The mother's casket alone. *Blackstone Collection.* Photograph $75-$100.

"United In Their Life Work. Re-United In Death." Interior view of double funeral. *Blackstone Collection.* Photograph $800-$1000.

Postmortem of young adult male. The ribbon on the floral arrangement just above the oval photograph says "OUR SON." Note coal stove in left corner. Photograph $50-$75.

This postmortem photograph was taken in Illinois and is dated 1927. *DiCenzo Collection.* $75-$100.

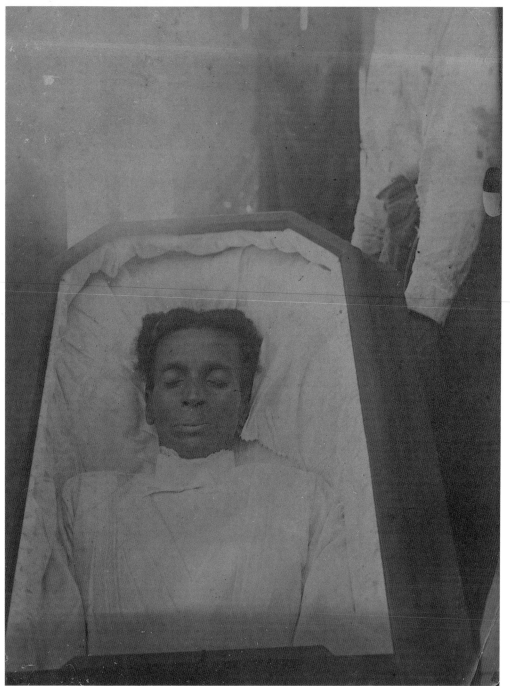

One of the most popular postmortem collectibles is that related to "Black Americana." Highly sought by collectors, these historical photographs are often considered rarities and have become expensive. *Blackstone Collection.* Photograph $300-$400.

"He died as he lived—a Christian." *DiCenzo Collection*. Photograph $75-$100.

"God saw that you were getting tired. And a cure was not to be, So He put His arms around you, And whispered, 'Come home with Me.' With tearful eyes we watched you suffer, And saw you fade away, Although we loved you dearly We could not make you stay. A golden heart stopped beating, A determined spirit was at rest, God broke our hearts to prove to us He only takes the best." *DiCenzo Collection*. Photograph $75-$100.

"Gone, but not forgotten." *DiCenzo Collection*. Photograph $75-$100.

119

"His memory is blessed." *DiCenzo Collection*.
Photograph $75-$100.

"A friend to his country and a believer in Christ." *DiCenzo Collection*. Photograph $75-$100.

"Dear Dad." *Groves Collection*.
Photograph $75-$100.

120

An elaborate velvet curtain and canopy provide the backdrop for this postmortem photograph. *Groves Collection.* Photograph $75-$100.

"Do not stand at my grave and weep; I am not there; I do not sleep. I am a thousand winds that blow; I am the diamond glints on snow; I am the gentle autumn's rain. When you awaken in the morning's hush, I am the swift uplifting rush. Of quiet birds in circled flight; I am the soft star that shines at night. Do not stand at my grave and cry. I am not there; I did not die." (author unknown) *Groves Collection.* Photograph $75-$100.

"His memory is blessed." *Neill Collection.* Photograph $75-$100.

121

"The Lord is my shepherd, I shall not want." *Neill Collection.* Photograph $75-$100.

"In Loving Remembrance." *Neill Collection.* Photograph $75-$100.

"Blessed are the pure in heart; for they shall see God." James Brady Hucle died in 1947, buried Union Cemetery, Columbus, Ohio. *Courtesy Jackie Weiner.* NFS.

"Eternal rest grant to him, O Lord! And let perpetual light shine on him." A set of two photographs showing the same deceased individual. *Private Collection*. Photographs $75-$100 each.

"Dear Father." Richmond, Indiana. *Private Collection*. Photograph $75-$100.

"Dearest brother, thou hast left us, Here, thy loss we deeply feel, But 'tis God that hath bereft us, He can all our sorrows heal." Chicopee, Massachusetts. *Private Collection*. Photograph $75-$100.

"Resting in hope of a glorious resurrection." *Private Collection*. Photograph $75-$100.

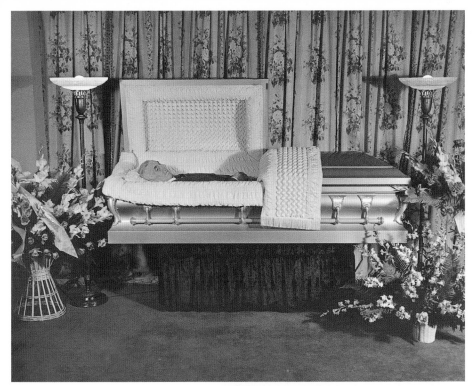

"At Peace." Hillsdale, Illinois. *Private Collection*. Photograph $75-$100.

"Father." Akron, Ohio. *Private Collection*. Photograph $75-$100.

"How desolate our home, bereft of thee." California, Pennsylvania. *Private Collection*. Photograph $75-$100.

"Daddy." Columbus, Ohio. *Private Collection.* $125-$150.

"Father." This is an excellent example of interior home decorating. *Private Collection.* $125-$150.

"Although he sleeps. His memory doth live. And cheering comfort. To his mourners give." Cleveland, Ohio. *Private Collection.* Photograph $125-$150.

"Rest in Peace." *Private Collection.* $125-$150.

"Our Dear Brother." *Private Collection.* $125-$150.

"God gave, He took, He will restore." *Private Collection*. $175-$200.

"He is not dead, but sleepeth." *Private Collection*. Photograph $175-$200.

Harold Raymond Featherstone monument in West Union St. Cemetery, Athens, Ohio (see next page). His father Clyde R. was born in 1894 and died in 1969; his mother Leah G. was born in 1894 and died in 1983. *Courtesy Carolyn McGuire.*

Harold Raymond Featherstone, son of C.R. and L.G. Griffin Featherstone, 1917-1919, buried West Union St. Cemetery, Athens, Ohio. Found behind the original photograph was the original obituary, transcribed below. *Private Collection.* Photograph $1000-$1200.

Obituary

Harold Raymond Featherstone, son of Clyde R. and Leah Griffin Featherstone was born, February 9, 1917 at Stewart, Ohio and died September 16, 1919 at Athens, Ohio. His age was two years, seven months and seven days. As a very young child he had been ill a great deal, but he had completely recovered from his earlier troubles and became quite robust and healthy.

Late on Tuesday afternoon he was accidentally drowned by falling into a cistern which had been left partly uncovered unbeknown to his parents.

Although his body was in the water only a very short time it was impossible to revive him. It was a terrible shock and irreparable loss to his parents, as he was the only child and will be therefore all the more greatly missed.

He was an attractive little fellow, full of life and energy. He was known by many outside his own family circle and loved by all who knew him. He was a very affectionate, loving little boy and easily won a place in the hearts of all who saw him.

Said Samuel Rogers in one of his writings: "Pointing to such, well might Cornelia say. When the rich casket shone in bright array. These are my jewels, well of such as he. When Jesus spake, well might his language be Suffer these little ones o come to me."

We wish to express our sincerest thanks to our many friends for their kindness shown us during our sad bereavement in the loss of our darling little boy; also the friends who sent beautiful floral offerings, Rev. Strecker for his kind words, and Mr. and Mrs. Walburn for their services. Mr. and Mrs. C.R. Featherstone.

"Weep not, father and mother, for me, For I am waiting in glory for thee." *S.L. Davis Collection.* Photograph $75-$100.

"Sleep on, sweet babe, and take thy rest, God called thee home, he thought it best." *S.L. Davis Collection.* Photograph $75-$100.

"A little flower of love. That blossomed but to die; Transplanted now above, To bloom with God on high." Rochester, New York. Note the glassware in the china cabinet to the left. *S.L. Davis Collection.* Photograph $75-$100.

130

"In heaven there is one angel more." Ralph Edmund Huffer, born January 13, 1920, died April 24, 1920. Parents, Ralph and Edan Euchle Huffer. *Courtesy Jackie Weiner*. NFS.

Ralph Edmund Huffer is buried in a single grave space, number 1006, section 72 in "Baby Land," Green Lawn Cemetery, Columbus, Ohio.

131

"Suffer little children to come unto me." *S.L. Davis Collection.* Photograph $75-$100.

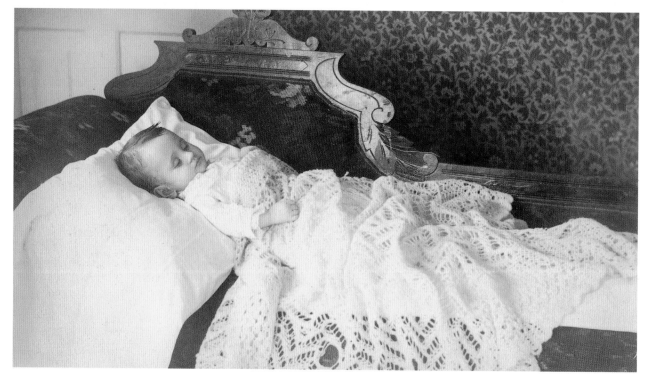

"A little time on earth he spent, Till God for him His angel sent." Elgin, Illinois, 1883. *S.L. Davis Collection.* Photograph $125-$150.

"Another little angel. Before the heavenly throne." *Blackstone Collection.* Photograph $1000-$1200.

"Weep not, father and mother, for me, For I am waiting in glory for thee." Houtzdale, Pennsylvania. *S.L. Davis Collection.* Photograph $500-$600.

"Our Darling." Washington Court House, Ohio. *S.L. Davis Collection*. Photograph $125-$150.

We have celebrated the lives of those shown throughout this publication.

"A precious one from us has gone." A family at the grave site of a loved one. *Blackstone Collection.* Photograph $100-$150.

Part 6

Postcards

Main entrance to Cemetery, Hicksville, Ohio.

Main entrance to Cemetery, Hicksville, Ohio. $8-$10.

"The cemetery has a two-fold mission in the community. It must provide a permanent and inviolable resting place for those who have gone before, and it should be so beautiful in landscape and memorial art that it will become a source of consolation and inspiration to the living. The serene majesty of Nature should reach out to comfort the sorrowful and the beauty of memorial art should testify that this is not forgotten and forsaken ground, that here love, sentiment and devotion are permanently enshrined." *Memorial Extension Commission, Inc. ©1934.*

Postcards related to cemeteries or burial are presently plentiful. Many cards depict the entrances to various cemeteries, chapels, monuments of ornamental and architectural designs, or special events held in a cemetery. These colorful and often black and white postcards are moderate in price and can be found at paper shows, shops, malls, various auction websites, and yard sales. Postcards can range from $2.00 to $25.00 due to significant geographical differences and the buyer's desire.

Entrance to Oak Dale Cemetery, Urbana, Ohio. Dedicated 1856 in memory of Gene and Mrs. John H. Young. $8-$10.

Greenwood Cemetery, Zanesville, Ohio. $10-$15.

Entrance to West Lawn Cemetery, Canton, Ohio. 1906. $8-$10.

Cemetery View, Washington Court House, Ohio. 1911. $10-$15.

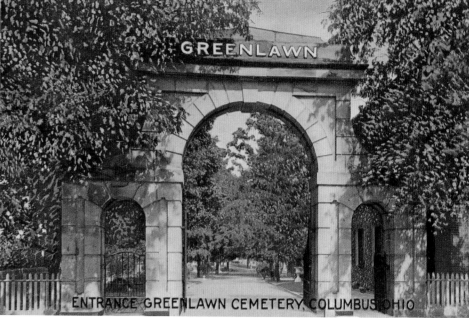

West Entrance, Green Lawn Cemetery, Columbus, Ohio. With over 360 acres, Green Lawn Cemetery is the second largest cemetery in the state of Ohio. It was established in 1848. $10-$15.

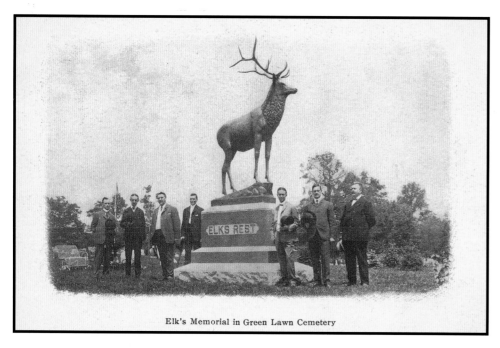

Elk's Memorial in Green Lawn Cemetery

Elk's Memorial in Green Lawn Cemetery, Columbus, Ohio. This memorial is no longer standing. $10-$15.

East Entrance, Green Lawn Cemetery, Columbus, Ohio. 1914. $8-$10.

Approach to Highland Cemetery, Ionia, Michigan. $8-$10.

Melrose Cemetery and Monument to the Grover Factory Victims,
Brockton, Massachusetts. 1906. $10-$15.

Old Potter Meeting House and Grave of Thomas Potter. Good Luck, New Jersey. 1907. $10-$15.

Gov. Bradford's Monument, Burial Hill. Governor of Plymouth Colony, 1621-1657, Plymouth, Massachusetts. $5-$10.

West Laurel Hill Cemetery. Chapel, Crematory and Columbarium for urn memorial. Bala-Cynwyd, Montgomery Co., Pennsylvania. $4-$6.

Old Cemetery, Lexington, Massachusetts. $10-$12.

The Mausoleum, Stanford University, California. $10-$15.

Entrance to Burial Hill, Plymouth, Massachusetts. 1908. $5-$10.

141

Gateway, Metairie Cemetery, New Orleans, Louisiana. $10-$15.

The Elk's Mausoleum, Greenwood Cemetery, New Orleans, Louisiana. The back reads: "This splendid tomb erected in 1912 under the administration of Exalted Ruler W.C. Murphy is located in Greenwood Cemetery, at the head of Canal Street. The tomb is built of Georgia white marble and is surmounted by a life size bronze Elk. The incipiency of the movement that brought about the building of the tomb is due to Mr. J.J. Lea. The insignia of the order is a striking feature of the tomb and all persons can see the clock face with its hands at 11 o'clock, reminding all Elks to think of their absent brothers, whether in the land of the living or in the Grand Lodge above." $8-$10.

Old St. Louis Cemetery, New Orleans, Louisiana. The back reads: "The most interesting of New Orleans historic burial places, the St. Louis Cemetery No. 1— there are three—has been in use for 175 years, with some of the inscriptions still decipherable dated 1800. Here lies the bodies of Paul Morphy, the famous chess player; Gayarre, the historian; Etienne de Bore, who first made granulated sugar; Charles LaSalle, brother of the famous explorer." $15-$18.

Entrance to Springdale Cemetery, Peoria, Illinois. $8-$10.

"A Drive in Bonaventure, Savannah, Ga." The back reads: "Bonaventure Cemetery [i]s famous wherever Savannah is known for its moss hung arching live oaks, camellias, wisteria, and azaleas of every hue. Originally the colonial home of the distinguished Tattnall family, Bonaventure was converted into a cemetery in 1869 and is considered one of the unique spots in America." $20-$25.

Mt. Olivet Cemetery, North Detroit, Michigan. $8-$10.

Riverside Cemetery, Oshkosh, Wisconsin. $8-$10.

Corinth National Cemetery, Corinth, Mississippi. "Established in 1866 by an Act of Congress as a memorial shrine to the heroic dead of the Battle of Corinth, fought October 3rd and 4th, 1862, between a Confederate Army under the command of General Sterling Price and a Union army commanded by General W.S. Rosecrans." $5-$8.

The Lakes, Brookside Cemetery, Watertown, New York. 1921. $5-$8.

ENTRANCE CROWN HILL CEMETERY INDIANAPOLIS, IND.

Entrance Crown Hill Cemetery, Indianapolis, Indiana. 1919. $5-$8.

Administration Building, Oak Hill Cemetery, Evansville, Ind.

Administration Building, Oak Hill Cemetery, Evansville, Indiana. $5-$8.

Entrance to Fairview Cemetery, Bluffton, Ind.

Entrance to Fairview Cemetery, Bluffton, Indiana. 1908. $5-$8.

Entrance to Oak Hill Cemetery, Evansville, Indiana. $5-$8.

Old Swedes Church, Wilmington, Delaware. 1909. $10-$12.

Blocher Monument, Forest Lawn Cemetery, Buffalo, New York. 1917. $8-$10.

67237-N

Lincoln Monument, Oak Ridge Cemetery, Springfield, Illinois. The back reads: "The foundation for the tomb was laid in 1869 and the superstructure was completed in 1871 at a cost of $180,000. In 1901 it was rebuilt at a cost of $100,000 and in 1931 an appropriation of $175,000 was voted to rebuild the structure. The obelisk rises 117 feet above the sidewalk and the base of the structure is seventy feet square and fifteen feet high. The monument contains the bodies of Abraham Lincoln—16th President of the U.S.A.—Mrs. Lincoln and three of the four Lincoln children." $5-$8.

Andrews Raiders Monument, National Cemetery, Chattanooga, Tenn. 1907. $10-$12.

"Boston, Mass., Grave of Franklin." Central monument printed with the name "FRANKLIN" surrounded by weathered headstones that appear to lean and cramp the central monument. $8-$10.

147

"Cemetry Bakersfield, Vt." 1910. $5-$8.

Foreign postcard. $10-$12.

The Geo. H. Long Mortuary, Kansas City, Kansas. *Courtesy Ann Davis.* $5-$8.

Chapel, Lakewood Cemetery, Minneapolis, Minnesota. 1912. $5-$8.

Black and white photographic postcard of a special event, location unknown. $8-$10.

Black and white photographic postcard of monuments, location unknown. Also see the "Monuments" section in Part 4 of this publication. $8-$10.

Black and white photographic postcard of unveiling of monument, location unknown. Dated May 30th 1912. $15-$20.

Black and white photographic postcard of memorial to FATHER. $5-$8.

Black and white photographic postcard of a parade with cemetery in background, location unknown. $15-$20.

Black and white 1920s photographic postcard of bereaved family members at a grave site in Estonia. $15-$20.

Black and white photographic postcard of bereaved Estonian family with deceased child. $20-$25.

Black and white 1920s photographic postcard from Estonia showing infant boy. Back of card indicates that the card was sent to an aunt from her brother in memory of cousin. $25-$30.

Black and white photographic postcard of infant child from Estonia, surrounded by flowers. $18-$20.

Black and white photographic postcard of a family posed at the base of a large monument, location unknown. $5-$10.

Scallop edge black and white photographic postcard of Estonian funeral procession and hearse. $20-$25.

Black and white photographic postcard of a family member in black mourning dress visiting a grave site covered in blooming peony bushes. Location unknown. $15-$20.

Black and white photographic postcard of small child in a "Whole Couch" casket surrounded by numerous floral arrangements, location unknown. Note the small child's rocker. $20-$25.

Black and white photographic postcard of majestic monuments, location unknown. $10-$15.

Black and white photographic postcard of "Mrs. Daniels" in "Half Couch" casket surrounded by floral arrangements. $20-$25.

Black and white photographic postcard of closed casket with floral arrangements, taken in a home. $10-$15.

PLEASE, MISS, GIVE ME HEAVEN (2). "If you please, Miss, give me Heaven, for my Mamma's there. You will find her with the Angels on the golden stair; She'll be glad it's me who's speaking, call her, won't you, please? For I want to surely tell her we're lonely here."

IF YOU PLEASE, MISS, GIVE ME HEAVEN (3). "When the girl received this message, Coming o'er the telephone, How her heart thrilled in that moment, And the wires seemed to moan; I will answer, just to please her, Yes, dear heart, I'll soon come home; Kiss me Mamma, kiss your darling, Through the telephone."

These three colorful postcards are part of a series. PLEASE, MISS, GIVE ME HEAVEN (1). "Papa. I'm so sad and lonely," sobbed a tearful little child. Since dear Mamma's gone to heaven, Papa, you've not smiled; I will speak to her, and tell her that we want her to come home; Just you listen, and I'll call her through the telephone." *Courtesy Mike and Cindy Schneider.* $15-$20 set.

155

Entrance to Floral Hill Cemetery, Hoopeston, Illinois. Floral Hill Cemetery was established in 1871, plotted by Alba Honeywell. Improvements were made in 1939 under Wm. M. Beggs, Mayor. *Courtesy of Karen and Sadie Evans.*

Appendix
Care of Collectible Documents

Original paper documents have become collectible and are readily available at most antique or paper shows, as well as through the eBay auction site. Many dealers specialize in old advertisements and documents and often have a good knowledge of their subject material. The original advertisements and documents shown throughout this publication range in price from $2 to $50 per item. The more rare the document, the more costly.

Many collectors of historical paper items do not realize that their collection could be in danger. It is important to become aware of the "enemies of paper" and seek professional advice in preserving paper items. For example, it is not wise to place valuable paper items in plastic storage bags purchased from a local grocery store, although this practice is often seen at various shows. If you purchase such an item, remove it from the bag as soon as possible (if moisture develops inside the bag, your valuable paper item may become worthless). Postcards should be kept in clear plastic sleeving, which allows the card's front and back to be visible through the plastic and discourages direct handling of the card. This sleeving can be purchased reasonably at local paper advertisement shows in your area.

Never subject paper collectibles to direct sunlight, which will cause fading. Acid burn can occur from wood, wood pulp mats, backings, and cardboard. Ultraviolet light causes colors and inks to fade. Infrared light accelerates aging, causing brittleness and discoloration. Permanent mounts, including dry mounting, wet mounting, and most glues and tapes, cause permanent and irreversible damage. Improper framing causes and encourages all of the above.

The greatest danger to your paper items comes from insects that like to feed on them. The older the paper, the greater the risk. Remember that paper collectibles retain their greatest value in pristine condition; anything that happens to change the condition of the item reduces its value. Protect your investment and avoid the enemies of paper.

Bibliography

Baker, MD, Roger D. *Postmortem Examination Specific Methods and Procedures.* Philadelphia & London: W.B. Saunders Company, 1967.

Canadian Funeral Service, Toronto, Canada, Vol. 20, No. 7, July 1942.

Illinois Funeral Directors Association, 1970. Published by the Illinois Funeral Directors Association.

Jackson, Percival E. *The Law of Cadavers and of Burial and Burial Places, Second Edition.* New York: Prentice-Hall, Inc., 1950.

Marion, John Francis. *Famous and Curious Cemeteries.* New York: Crown Publishers, Inc., 1977.

Mayer, J. Sheridan. *Restorative Art.* Cincinnati, Ohio: Paula Publishing Co., Inc., 1980.

Renouard, Augustus. *Undertakers' Manual, Second Edition.* Rochester, N.Y.: A.H. Nirdlinger & Co.

Sasnett, J. Randolph. *Living Memorials.* Stone & Pierce, © MCMXLVII.

Spriggs, A.O. *The Art and Science of Embalming.* Springfield, Ohio and Leaside, Ontario: The Champion Company, 1948.

Wright, Sewell P. *Ethical Advertising for Funeral Directors.* Trade Periodical Company, © 1924.

Index